Russell Ash is best known as the author of the
annual *Top 10 of Everything* and other popular
reference books. He has also compiled numerous
humour books, including *The Cynic's Dictionary*,
Howlers and *The Uncensored Boy's Own* and is
the co-author of *Bizarre Books*. His first foray
into unusual names was *Potty, Fartwell & Knob:
Extraordinary But True Names of British People*,
followed by *Busty, Slag and Nob End: Remarkably
Rude But real Names of People, Places and Products
from all Over the World.*

Potty, Fartwell & Knob
'It may well make you laugh like a hyena.'
Independent

'Hilariously brilliant... I cried with laughter... I love
this book.'
Amazon customer review

Busty, Slag and Nob End
'You will laugh out loud, but might be slightly
embarrassed for doing so.'
The Sunday Times

'Wickedly, deliciously funny... Outrageously
hilarious... One of the funniest books ever!!'
Amazon customer review

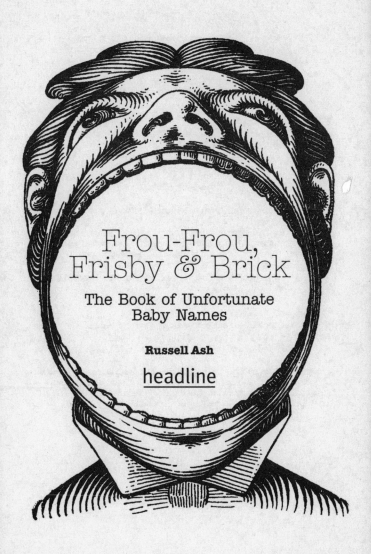

Frou-Frou, Frisby & Brick

The Book of Unfortunate Baby Names

Russell Ash

<u>headline</u>

First published in 2010
by HEADLINE PUBLISHING GROUP

1

Cataloguing in Publication Data is available from the British Library

978 0 7553 6088 8

Designed by Fiona Andreanelli (www.andreanelli.com)

Printed and bound in Great Britain by Clays Ltd, St Ives plc

Headline's policy is to use papers that are natural, renewable and
recyclable products and made from wood grown in sustainable
forests. The logging and manufacturing processes are expected to
conform to the environmental regulations of the country of origin.

HEADLINE PUBLISHING GROUP
An Hachette UK Company
338 Euston Road
London NW1 3BH

www.headline.co.uk
www.hachette.co.uk
www.russellash.com

Contents

Introduction

In the beginning

As the author of *Potty, Fartwell & Knob* (or *Morecock, Fartwell & Hoare*, as it is known in the USA), *Busty, Slag and Nob End* and *Big Pants, Burpy and Bumface*, I have perhaps been more exposed than most to the oddities of personal names and naming. In the course of my research, it occurred to me that every first name in those books resulted from some positive decision on the part of one or both parents. The fact that I, and thousands of readers, found them funny suggested that many parents had made unwise choices and that a self-help book was called for. There are plenty of books offering advice on what you might call your baby, many of them focusing on the meanings of names – but since most people don't even know the meaning of their own names, that seems a minor consideration. Much more to the point: is the name likely to cause your child problems and make him or her unhappy in their future life?

Since few books offer counsel on this important issue, *Frou-Frou, Frisby & Brick* aims to fill that gap. It is a manual, a *vade mecum*, that presents a range of real examples. Anyone with too much time on their hands could cobble together a list of silly names that no one in their right minds could ever bestow on their baby, but I have chronicled exclusively cases where someone did – and in every instance with the official provenance to prove it. Even allowing for the possibility that some names may have entered the records as the result of a mistake on the part of a registrar who misheard, or have been transcribed from a semi-legible census return, it leaves us with an enormous catalogue of 'strange but true' names – and its many awful warnings from history on what *not* to call your baby.

Miss Demeanours

A lot has to do with foresight. Who would be thinking that far ahead when baby daughter lies gurgling in her cot? But when she grows up she may be addressed as 'Miss' or some other title: there have been a number of Miss Demeanours, not to mention Miss Adventures, Anthropes, Behaves, Conceptions, Fortunes, Haps, Heards, Takes and Tresses, as well as a Mrs Sippi or two. Likewise, for boys, a multitude of Master Bates, Minds, Pieces, Races and Spies, a Mister Totally (though, sadly, no Mister Completely) and, for all I know, a Sir Loin and a Lord Loveaduck. Since we are generally stuck with our surnames, such outcomes are unavoidable, but parents with certain surnames have to be especially careful in their choice of first name. As we shall see, part of the problem is lack of thought in imagining the effect of the first name's being used as an initial or in combination with the surname, so that some unforeseen and unfortunate juxtaposition or *double entendre* emerges. It must be admitted that certain surnames don't go with anything, but that's no reason to make it worse by teaming it with a silly first name.

You called him *what*?

The tensions and euphoria of childbirth, perhaps combined with the after-effects of an epidural, may well account for some of the more bizarre naming decisions as all reason goes to the wind: how else does one account for the naming decision of the Ducks who called their son Chris P., or the Peacocks who elicited the question, 'You called him *what*?!' after giving their son the immortal name Drew Peacock? Since, unlike financial and other transactions, the registration of a baby's name does not permit a 'cooling-off' period during which over-hasty naming decisions can be overturned, Crispy Duck and Droopy Cock (sorry, Chris P. Duck and Drew Peacock) are the names by which they will be known for the rest of their lives. Of course, women have the opportunity to change their surnames by marriage, although there is an equal opportunity to trade a 'normal' name for a far worse one. Any adult can change their name by deed poll – but as the examples here testify, even those are sometimes beyond bizarre.

Common as Muck

There are dishes that are described on menus as 'local speciality', which you never encounter anywhere else. There is a reason: they are usually awful. The same principle applies to baby names: do not be tempted by names that no one has ever used before – your son or daughter will not thank you for having to spend the rest of their life spelling it out, explaining its origin and justifying why they are so called. In attempting to avoid the commonplace (as Sam Goldwyn reputedly remarked, 'Why did you name him Sam? Every Tom, Dick and Harry is named Sam!'), or offer their child the chance to stand apart from their peers, parents often come up with something so peculiar that their offspring will never live it down. They forget, perhaps, that as they attempt to make their child different, what most kids really want is to be the same: those who look or behave differently, or who have names that can be mocked or turned into some memorable nickname, are the ones who are bullied. However much you think you are being clever and original, imagine, just for a nanosecond, how your child will be treated at school if he bears the name Poke Sharpley, Singular Onion Gallehawk, Heidi High or Mucky Haddock, and you will see what I mean.

So bad they named them twice

However proud you may be of your family name, do not give it to your child as a first name. There are fictional examples, such as Major Major in Joseph Heller's *Catch-22*, whose father deviously claims he has named him Caleb, and who rises through the ranks to become a figure of fun as Major Major Major – but there are plenty of real ones. Neville Neville, the father of footballers Gary and Phil Neville, is not the only person to have his surname repeated as his first name: real-life examples encompass Goody Goody (born Nottingham, *c.*1567), Bold Bold (married Hampshire, 1819), Daisy Daisy (born Lancashire, 1880) and, not least, James Bottom Bottom Bottom (born Yorkshire, 1852), who I featured in *Potty, Fartwell & Knob*, leading the three-year-old daughter of musician friends to march around the house obsessively singing his remarkable repetitious name. Reduplicative names attract attention but are, frankly, usually very silly.

Historical or hysterical?

Names that commemorate some national event or a celebrity or hero of the day are bound to date. Consider poor Liberal Reform Darby (born Essex, 1850) or Trafalgar Brattle [*sic*] (born Kent, 1870), and all those little Adolfs of the 1930s. Project into the future and imagine how you will explain to your child why you called him or her Jedward, Piers Morgan, Osama Bin, Subo or X. Factor. Placing 'De', 'La' or 'Ty' in front, 'isha' at the end or an apostrophe in some unlikely place emerged from rap culture and may be of the moment, but what happens when that moment passes?

A funny spell

Weird spellings – Berhty, Phran, Bil, Charleigh, Shardonnay, Barbora and Melodi – are equally risky in that your child will get off to a bad start if he or she is constantly correcting the teacher's spelling. The same applies to more 'traditional' British names with counter-intuitive pronunciation, such as Cholmondeley, Cockburn, Colquhoun, Dalziel, Looney, Mainwaring, Marjoribanks, St John, Wriothesley and others of that ilk: all have been used as first names, but think how bored your child will get spending his life complaining that his name is spelled like this, but pronounced like that. Not giving babies names at all, just initials, is another current fad: AC and J appear among the most popular names in some US states, while in England and Wales twenty-three boys were registered as TJ and six as AJ in 2008.

It's the way you say them

Jokes are less funny the more you repeat them, hence you would be advised to avoid such whimsical conceits as naming your twins Kate and Duplicate (as did Mr and Mrs Ford of Williamson, Tennessee, USA, in 1908), Pete and Repeat or Arthur and Martha, as well as first names that rhyme with one's surname, like Mabel Abel, Ruth Booth, Danny Fanny, Hugh Glue, Polly Jolly, Peg Legg, Dick Prick, Hugh Pugh and Nellie Smellie and palindromes such as Mary Byram, Hannah Hannah, Revilo Oliver and Yendis Sidney. A further note of caution is to eschew names that sound like a statement (Wood Burns, Liza Wrong and so on) and names that could be those of a porn star or stripper (so forget about Hooters or Melons). On the other hand, you can't predict who your daughter might marry, and thus end up with a surname that fits awkwardly with her first name, or whether your child will end up in a profession that is laughably appropriate or inappropriate to their name (known in the trade as 'nominative determinism'). Since these possibilities are beyond parental control, they are not explored.

True Brits

In the UK, parents have frequently added odd names as middle names, including Marmite, Kiddie, Bovril and Spearmint, which were bizarrely briefly fashionable – as, indeed, was 'Bizarre'. Thus Harris Vole Candle (born Jersey, c.1820) could at least ignore Vole and just put up with the ridicule of being called 'Candle', while Isaac Worm Butcher (born Suffolk, 1843) could take his Worm out, as it were.

Certain first names appear to carry prejudicial baggage of which parents may be advised to steer clear. A 2009 survey investigated the names of children that teachers considered most likely to be disruptive:

Teachers' pests – Britain's naughtiest kids' names

	Boys	**Girls**
1	Callum	Chelsea
2	Connor	Courtney
3	Jack	Chardonnay
4	Daniel	Aleisha
5	Brandon	Casey
6	Charlie	Crystal
7	Kyle	Jessica
8	Liam	Brooke
9	Jake	Demi
10	Brooklyn	Aisha

Pet names are another no-go area – not that you meet a lot of people called Rover or Tiddles – but these days the names given to the family dog or cat are just as likely to be those of a person and are therefore best avoided unless you want to call your child in the playground only to find a large labrador bounding towards you:

Man's 10 best friends

1 Max
2 Molly
3 Sam / Sammy
4 Meg / Megan
5 Ben
6 Holly
7 Charlie
8 Oscar
9 Barney
10 Millie / Milly

Photo Gunn & Co.
Ltd., Richmond. Beauty and the Beast. Autotype

It works both ways: based on a survey of dogs
and cats treated at the PDSA's forty-seven PetAid
hospitals, these are the celebrities whose names
are considered most appropriate for the family pet:

Top 10 celebrity pet names in the UK

1 Tyson (Mike)
2 Harry (Potter or Prince)
3 Ozzy (Osbourne)
4 Robbie (Williams)
5 Rooney (Wayne)
6 Beckham (David)
7 Paris (Hilton)
8 Elvis (Presley)
9 Jessie (Wallace – Kat Slater in *EastEnders*)
10 Britney (Spears)

American appellations

The inclusion of American names should not be taken as implying that they are in any way stranger than British names (although some are), but the presence of many immigrants – whose names, while not unusual in their countries of origin, often sound odd to an ear unused to hearing them – adds an extra dimension and source – and, of course, there are a lot more of them to choose from. As previously noted, there may be good reasons for ignoring rare names, and for American parents the US Social Security Administration helpfully indicates these by publishing surveys of the most and least popular first names in the United States – least being those featuring at the bottom of a table of the top 1,000, hence, for example, when in the 1880s 91,673 girls were called Mary, a mere thirty-nine received the name Eura:

The 10 least popular first names in the USA, 1880s

	Boys	**Girls**
1	Ammon	Eura
2	Ewald	Missie
3	Brice	Biddie
4	Linton	Mannie
5	Vester	Libby
6	Reinhold	Johannah
7	Ewing	Leana
8	Stanton	Media
9	Moody	Hertha
10	Kelley	Reta

A comparative survey for the period 2000–08 revealed the following:

The 10 least popular first names in the USA, 2000–08

	Boys	**Girls**
1	Jax	Finley
2	Heriberto	Beatrice
3	Stephon	Dasia
4	Daryl	Zara
5	Krish	Jaslene
6	Zayne	Myla
7	Deonte	Charlie
8	Vincenzo	Ireland
9	Jakobe	Diane
10	Lucian	Marely

Recent research conducted by Professor David Kalist of Shippensburg University, Pennsylvania, published in *Social Science Quarterly* appears to indicate that certain first names, based on a study of more than 15,000, predispose their bearers to lead lives of crime. Whether this results from a bias against certain names, so that those who bear them are subjected to bullying and turn to crime, or other factors, remains unproven.

Top 10 'criminal' boys' names in the USA*

1 Alec
2 Ernest
3 Garland
4 Ivan
5 Kareem
6 Luke
7 Malcolm
8 Preston
9 Tyrell
10 Walter

* Listed alphabetically

World wide weird

Curious names are not exclusively an
Anglo-American phenomenon. In 1996
a court in Sweden rejected the name
Brfxxccxxmnpcccclllmmnprxvclmnckssqlbb11116
(allegedly pronounced 'Albin') and in 2004 Sara
Leisten of Gothenburg was refused permission to call
her son Staalman, the Swedish for Superman, even
though the registration office had allowed the names
Tarzan and Batman. In 2008 the press reported that
a girl in New Zealand was made a ward of court so
that she could change her name from Talula Does
The Hula From Hawaii. The country's courts had
previously intervened to ban such names as Sex
Fruit, Keenan Got Lucy, Satan, Yeah Detroit and Hitler,
but, it was claimed, Number 16 Bus Shelter, Violence
and Midnight Chardonnay had been allowed, as had
twins Benson and Hedges and Fish and Chips, while
a couple who had been prevented from giving their
baby the name 4Real opted for Superman instead.
Good job they didn't live in Sweden.

Russell Ash
Lewes, 2010
www.russellash.com

Note: All locations of births, marriages, deaths, etc. are England
and Wales unless otherwise stated; all census records are
England unless otherwise stated.

How Could They?

E very generation has produced its share of names that departed from the ordinary, but these are some of the most extreme and rarest – in some instances unique – examples. They range from Puritan names (Abuse-not, Fly-fornication, et al) dating back to the sixteenth century to their counterparts in hippy culture in the 1960s, when babies were regularly called such names as Alchemy, Andromeda, Aquamarine and Avatar. Out of these have emerged many of the increasingly bizarre names favoured by today's celebrities and countless others, many of which are made doubly strange by the surname with which they are combined.

Aberycusgentylis	**Aberycusgentylis Balthropp**, baptized Iver, Buckinghamshire, 25 January 1648
Abishag	**Abishag Doxey**, died Ashbourne, Derbyshire, 1854
Absolutely	**Absolutely Nobody**, born 7 January 1957; died Seattle, Washington, USA, 26 October 1993
Abstinence	**Abstinence Pougher**, baptized St Nicholas, Leicester, 30 June 1672
Abuse-not	**Abuse-not Ellis**, baptized Warbleton, Sussex, 17 September 1592
Accepted	**Accepted Frewen**, baptized Northiam, Sussex, 26 May 1588; died 28 March 1664. *Accepted Frewen, brother of Thankfull Frewen (born Northiam, Sussex, 1591; died 1656), became Archbishop of York.*

Addenda	**Addenda Morse**, born Kentucky, *c.*1865 (Lewis, Kentucky, 1870 US census). *Addenda ('addition') had a sister called Appends ('added').*
Addition	**Addition Lang**, born Ontario, Canada, 1 July 1896. *Addition was the fifth child of farmer Garrett and Ellen Lang – who then had three more, including twins James and Theresa.*
Adora	**Adora Ball**, born Michigan, *c.*1855 (Burt, Michigan, 1860 US census)
Aeronaut	**Aeronaut Hayes**, born Lincoln, *c.*1865 (Lincoln, 1881 census)
Affability	**Affability Box**, baptized St John Horsleydown, Bermondsey, London, 3 March 1822
Agent	**Agent Mildred Allsop**, born Barrow upon Soar, Leicestershire, 1904
Agony	**Agony Minchin**, born Bradfield, Berkshire, 1860
Ah	**Ah Choo**, married Stepney, London, 1882
	Ah Fuck, born China, *c.*1829 (Drytown, California, 1860 US census)
Alabama	**Alabama Hammer**, born 11 February 1913; died Ardmore, Oklahoma, USA, April 1984
Albino	**Albino White**, married Hackney, London, 1907
Alien	**Alien Fly**, born 4 May 1902; died Jackson, Tennessee, USA, 1 June 1994
All	**All Done**, born Derby, 1898
Alphabeta	**Alphabeta Swithinbank**, died Hunslet, Yorkshire, 1849

Amaziah	**Amaziah Swallow**, married Asenath Cumings, Dunstable, Massachusetts, USA, 18 January 1810
Angry	**Angry Howard**, born 1 May 1892; died Louisiana, USA, August 1965
Anonymous	**Anonymous Prober**, born Texas, c.1909 (Mason, Texas, 1910 US census)
Any	**Any Day**, born Barningham, Suffolk, c.1857 (Crawshawbooth, Lancashire, 1871 census)
Armageddon	**Armageddon Danbury Margerum**, born East Stonehouse, Devon, 1875 (Raunds, Northamptonshire, 1881 census)
Arsabella	**Arsabella Bending**, born Payhembury, Devon, c.1818 (Feniton, Devon, 1851 census)
Arsenal	**Arsenal Berriball Prout**, born Tavistock, Cornwall, 1845
Arsenic	**Arsenic Borwoski**, born New York, USA, 30 October 1895
Arsfona	**Arsfona Bumgardner**, born West Virginia, c.1885 (Williams, West Virginia, 1920 US census)
Arson	**Arson Skidmore**, married Gloucester, 1849
Asad	**Asad Experience Wilson**, born 1895; died Wasco, Oregon, USA, 3 November 1946
Asbo	**Asbo Fitch**, born Chicago, Illinois, c.1860 (Chicago, 1920 US census). *Non-Brits may wish to know that an ASBO is an Anti-Social Behaviour Order, a civil order to prevent offenders from committing anti-social acts.*
Ashram	**Ashram Hayban**, born 14 March 1953; died New Jersey, USA, 2 March 2008

Asia	**Asia Minor**, born Pennsylvania, 1881 (Monongahela Township, Pennsylvania, 1900 US census)
Asse	**Asse Bollock**, born North Carolina, c.1850 (Pactolus, Pitt, North Carolina, 1880 US census)
Atomic	**Atomic Hill**, born 30 April 1946; died North Little Rock, Arkansas, USA, 29 August 2002
Au	**Au Revoir**, born St Giles, London, 1887
Avagina	**Avagina Ledford**, born North Carolina, c.1832 (Cherokee, North Carolina, 1850 US census)
Avast	**Avast Price**, born 14 January 1919; died Monroe, North Carolina, USA, April 1974
Banger	**Banger Balster**, married Manchester, Lancashire, 1855

Banjo	**Banjo Thomas**, born Dudley, Worcestershire, c.1836 (Bloxwich, Staffordshire, 1871 census)
Bannastes	**Bannastes Naff**, born Lancashire, c.1821 (Whalley, Lancashire, 1841 census)
Baron	**Baron Tool**, married Scarborough, Yorkshire, 1855
Basha	**Basha Bollock** (female), born North Carolina, c.1849 (Pactolus, Pitt, North Carolina, 1880 US census)
Beaky	**Beaky Mace**, born 28 February 1929; died Surrey, 2001
Becautious	**Becautious Hunter**, born 28 May 1916; died Birmingham, Alabama, USA, 12 April 2009
Be-Courteous	**Be-Courteous Cole**, born Pevensey, Sussex, 1570
Bell	**Bell Ringer**, married Door, Wisconsin, USA, 20 August 1885
Bellend	**Bellend Cokella** (female), born Ireland, c.1840 (Ramsbottom, Lancashire, 1871 census)
Bendy	**Bendy Corner**, born Stoke Damerel, Devon, 1892
Best	**Best Splatt**, baptized Whitestone, Devon, 2 July 1668
Big	**Big Ben**, born California, c.1835 (Lincoln, California, 1880 US census)
	Big Boy Johnson, died Ware, Georgia, USA, 23 December 1946
	Big Dick, born Nevada, c.1857 (Riddle, Idaho, 1930 US census)
	Big Head, born California, c.1857 (Fresno, California, 1860 US census)

Bijou	**Bijou Butt**, born Okehampton, Devon, *c.*1860 (Gloucester, 1891 census)
Bishop	**Bishop Fanny**, born Lutterworth, Leicestershire, 1844
Blacken	**Blacken White**, born Tennessee, *c.*1892 (Lawrence, Tennessee, 1920 US census)
Blandina	**Blandina Parody**, born Bedwelty, Monmouthshire, 1875
Blo	**Blo Job**, born Llanelli, Carmarthenshire, 1892
Blooming	**Blooming Alexander**, born Plymouth, Devon, *c.*1816 (Plymouth, 1851 census)
	Blooming Ice, born Alabama, *c.*1852 (Marshall, Alabama, 1860 US census)
Body	**Body Hunter**, married Daniel Nippers, Lincoln, Tennessee, USA, 24 June 1882
Bogey	**Bogey Boe**, born *c.*1812; passenger on *Emily*, Liverpool, UK–New York, USA, arrived 2 August 1932
Bogs	**Bogs Simons**, died Maidstone, Kent, 1853
Boileta	**Boileta Perks**, born Birmingham, Warwickshire, 1843
Bomb	**Bomb Gibson**, born Currie, Midlothian, *c.*1838 (Dunfermline, Fife, 1881 Scotland census)
Boney	**Boney Penile**, born North Carolina, USA, 6 October 1881; died 6 September 1954
Bosom	**Bosom Thaxter** (male), born Barningham, Norfolk, *c.*1811 (Gresham, Norfolk, 1851 census)
Botty	**Botty Brown**, born Bolton, Lancashire, *c.*1790 (Bolton, 1851 census)

Bounce	**Bounce E. Burbidge**, born Sheffield, Yorkshire, c.1856 (Sheffield, 1871 census)
Brown	**Brown Hatt**, born Bury, Lancashire, c.1842 (Musbury, Lancashire, 1871 census)
	Brown Rice, born 25 December 1907; died Gulfport, Mississippi, USA, December 1986
Bumon	**Bumon Boys**, born Cuba, c.1860 (New York, 1880 US census)
Burp	**Burp Bendon**, born Somerset, c.1771 (Old Cleeve, Somerset, 1841 census)
Burpy	**Burpy Loomer**, born Massachusetts, c.1869 (Brigton, Massachusetts, 1870 US census)
	Burpy Prouty, baptized Lancaster, Massachusetts, USA, 18 March 1764
Calamity	**Calamity Burkes**, born Arkansas, c.1900 (Union, Arkansas, 1910 US census)
Carnage	**Carnage Laverack**, born Selby, Yorkshire, 1877
Cash	**Cash Register**, born Florida, USA, 9 April 1946; died Burnsville, Texas, 19 February 1997
Celestial	**Celestial Rice**, born Ireland, c.1795 (Liverpool, Lancashire, 1861 census)
Cement	**Cement Blackband**, died Aston, Warwickshire, 1895
Changed	**Changed Collins**, born Brightling, Sussex, 1 January 1598. *She was the sister of Increased Collins.*
Charming	**Charming Frothingham**, born New York, USA, c.1882
Chase	**Chase Kuntz**, born Pennsylvania, c.1866 (Lancaster, Pennsylvania, 1920 US census)

Chesty	**Chesty Carroll** (male), born Dublin, Ireland, c.1847 (Rotherham, Yorkshire, 1861 census)
Chipman	**Chipman Fish**, married Betsey Howland, Sandwich, Massachusetts, USA, 11 February 1792
Chlorine	**Chlorine Daily**, born 24 October 1909; died Aquilla, Texas, USA, 16 October 1981
Christ	**Christ Bogoff**, born c.1885 (Akron, Ohio, 1930 US census)
Christmas	**Christmas Day**, baptized Lowestoft, Suffolk, 27 December 1762
	Christmas Holiday, married Ampthill, Bedfordshire, 1864
	Christmas Merry, born Williton, Somerset, 1885
	Christmas White, born Boston, Lincolnshire, 1858
Chrome	**Chrome Cox**, born Missouri, USA, 29 August 1884; died San Diego, California, 15 February 1955
Clammy	**Clammy Townend**, born Pontefract, Yorkshire, c.1877 (Golcar, Yorkshire, 1891 census)
Clotworthy	**Clotworthy Hoare**, born Kent, c.1837 (Blackheath, Kent, 1841 census)
Cocaine	**Cocaine Fisher**, born c.1876; died Clark, Missouri, USA, 31 March 1908
Colly	**Colly Flower**, father of Rebecca Flower, born 7 September 1797; baptized St Anne, Soho, London, 24 September 1797
Comet	**Comet Halley**, born Michigan, 10 July 1910; died Muskegon, Michigan, USA, 2 January 1976. *Halley's Comet was seen in 1910.*

Comfort	**Comfort Balls**, married Mitford, Norfolk, 1879
	Comfort Starr, born Ashford, Kentucky, America, 11 April 1624; died 30 October 1711
Confidence	**Confidence Klotz**, born 1 August 1908; died Red Bluff, California, USA, 4 August 2001
Conservative	**Conservative Hubbard**, born Ruskington, Lincolnshire, c.1839; died Sleaford, Lincolnshire, 1914

Conservator	**Conservator Lilo**, born Italy, c.1883 (Pittsburgh, Pennsylvania, 1910 US census)
Consider	**Consider Crapo**, born Illinois, c.1849 (Wexford, Michigan, 1880 US census)
Constant	**Constant Pain** (female), born Hackney, London, 1901 (Hackney, 1901 census)

Continent	**Continent Walker**, baptized Alfriston, Sussex, 22 December 1594
Cool	**Cool Joe Cool**, born 22 December 1945; died Desert Hot Springs, California, USA, 10 April 2008
Cowboy	**Cowboy Begay**, born 15 July 1904; died Kykotsmovi Village, Arizona, USA, July 1981
Cricket	**Cricket Batter**, born Missouri, 1894 (Prairie, Arkansas, 1900 US census)
Curley	**Curley Bush**, born Aldeburgh, Suffolk, c.1841 (Aldeburgh, 1851 census)
Cycle	**Cycle Cockwell**, born Plymouth, Devon, c.1888 (Plymouth, 1891 census)
	Cycle Herring, born Madeley, Shropshire, c.1897 (Shifnal, Shropshire, 1901 census)
Czar	**Czar Champagne**, born 12 November 1890; died Ogdensburg, New York, USA, November 1974
Czarina	**Czarina Podmore**, born Burslem, Staffordshire, c.1842 (Burslem, 1891 census)
Daily	**Daily Boner** (female), born Hernhill, Kent, c.1898 (Hernhill, 1901 census)
Damp	**Damp Jenkin**, born c.1781 (West Shefford, Berkshire, 1841 census)
Danger	**Danger Dangervil**, born 29 June 1943; died Homestead, Florida, USA, 23 November 2005
Dangerous	**Dangerous Bird**, born c.1879 (Montana, 1891 US Indian census)
Dansey	**Dansey Dansey**, baptized St Helen's, Worcester, 18 September 1800

Delicious	**Delicious Bacon**, born Georgia, 1895 (Reidsville Town, Georgia, 1900 US census)
Depression	**Depression Carter**, born North Carolina, c.1871 (Blues Sand Hill, North Carolina, 1910 US census)
Didimus	**Didimus Smalley**, born Lincoln, 1886
Diehappy	**Diehappy Badger**, born West Bromwich, Staffordshire, c.1860 (West Bromwich, 1861 census)
Dieter	**Dieter Burger**, born Illinois, c.1904 (Madison, Illinois, 1920 US census)
Dijonnaise	**Dijonnaise Rutledge**, born 10 July 1993; died Woodville, Mississippi, USA, 31 December 2008
Dildo	**Dildo Lunan**, born Canada, c.1846 (Palmer, Massachusetts, 1860 US census)
Diligence	**Diligence Constant**, buried St Peter upon Cornhill, London, 1 November 1724
Ding	**Ding Ding**, died Thanet, Kent, 30 April 1971
Discretion	**Discretion Watkinson**, married Elizabeth Wild, South Muskham, Nottinghamshire, 17 November 1659
Doctor	**Doctor Septimus Forrest**, born Preston, Lancashire, c.1834 (Blackburn, Lancashire, 1851 census). *Seventh sons were believed to have special powers, and were sometimes given the name 'Doctor', especially in Lancashire.*
Double	**Double Curry**, born Louisiana, c.1907 (Ouachita, Louisiana, 1910 US census)
Driver	**Driver Bus**, born Somerset, c.1879 (Leeds, Yorkshire, 1901 census)

Drug	**Drug Strange**, born Macon, Alabama, c.1847 (Jackson, Texas, 1860 US census)
Druid	**Druid Clodfelter**, born 29 August 1912; died Damascus, Maryland, USA, 1 March 2005
Dude	**Dude Dobbs**, born Mississippi, c.1888 (Chicago, Illinois, 1920 US census)
	Dude Sugarberg, born Mile End, London, c.1895 (Mile End, 1901 census)
Duke	**Duke Dyke**, born St Thomas, Devon, 1849
	Duke Earl, born Alabama, c.1905 (Riderwood, Alabama, 1930 US census)
Dusty	**Dusty Rhodes**, born 1940; died Wigan, Lancashire, 1999
Dynamite	**Dynamite Partee**, born North Carolina, c.1900 (Winston-Salem, North Carolina, 1930 US census)
Earless	**Earless Barber**, born 3 May 1897; died Lafayette, Tennessee, USA, May 1981
Early	**Early Bird**, married Phillips Harris, Colbert, Alabama, USA, 4 December 1881
Earth	**Earth Stone**, born Georgia, c.1867 (Alexander, Georgia, 1920 US census)
Earwacker	**Earwacker Deadman**, born Alton, Hampshire, 1849
Easter	**Easter Bunny**, born Yorkshire, c.1826 (Bradford, Yorkshire, 1841 census)
	Easter Noodle, born Georgia, c.1874 (Rose Creek, Georgia, 1880 US census)
Easy	**Easy Pease**, died Billericay, Essex, 1889

Eatme	**Eatme Blechart**, born *c*.1861 (Montpelier, Idaho, 1930 US census)
	Eatme Edwards, born *c*.1827 (Amlwch, Anglesey, 1841 Wales census)
Eclipse	**Eclipse Green**, born Mississippi, *c*.1877 (Yazoo, Mississippi, 1880 US census)
Ecolastica	**Ecolastica Arse**, baptized Santa Lucia, Macari, Peru, 9 February 1886
Elastic	**Elastic Eggins**, born 17 February 1956; died Houston, Texas, USA, January 2001
	Elastic Scott, died Montgomery, Alabama, USA, 28 December 1958
Electric	**Electric Ball**, born Virginia, 1894 (Elk Garden, Virginia, 1900 US census)
Elmadorus	**Elmadorus Nothing Sprinkle**, born Virginia, USA, *c*.1810; died March 1888. *Elmadorus Nothing Sprinkle, a hatter, had one daughter, Memphis Tappon, with his first wife, and with his second, Martha, née McCollum (born Scotland, c.1833), two sons, to whom they gave the names Myrtle Ellmore and Onyx Curren, and six daughters, Empress Vandalia, Tatnia Zain, Okinna Maletta, Ogwilt, Agawith and Wintosse Emmah.*
Embryo	**Embryo Damocles Pamenter**, born Shoreditch, London, 1900
Emperor	**Emperor Adrian**, born St James, Clerkenwell Green, London, 7 May 1809
Endeavour	**Endeavour Eugene Williams**, resident of Queensland, Australia, 1913 (Australian electoral rolls, 1903–1954). *Since it was revealed in 1997 in the TV series of Colin Dexter's Inspector Morse that Morse's first name was 'Endeavour', more than twenty British babies have received it as a middle name.*

Energy	**Energy Ward**, married Mary Coker, St Albans, Hertfordshire, 15 October 1863
Enormous	**Enormous Little**, born c.1950; died Shelby, North Carolina, USA, 24 November 2007
Enough	**Enough Wright**, born Shropshire, c.1835 (South Bradford, Shropshire, 1841 census). *Charles and Margret [sic] Wright named their eighth son 'Enough' – but then had another, Moses, and a daughter, Mary.*
Epaphroditus	**Epaphroditus Marsh**, baptized Hannington, Wiltshire, 23 January 1636. *His brothers were called Narcissus and Onesiphorus.*
Epenetus	**Epenetus Earwaker**, born St Saviour, Southwark, London, 1871
Epiphany	**Epiphany Bullock**, born Lanivet, Cornwall, 1861
	Epiphany Bullock Cock, born St Austell, Cornwall, 1844
	Epiphany Lullaby, married Veryan, Cornwall, 3 January 1767
E. Pluribus Unum	**E. Pluribus Unum Medsker**, married Lone Rush (born Owen, Gosport, Indiana; died 1963), Morgan, Indiana, USA, 14 September 1911. *'E pluribus unum', Latin for 'Out of many, one', is the motto of the United States.*
Erect	**Erect Davis**, born New York, c.1848 (Plymouth, New York, 1850 US census)
Errata	**Errata Ford**, born Indiana, c.1880 (Washington, Indiana, 1880 US census). *'Errata', a list of mistakes, such as those in a book, was the name given to the youngest of the six children of farm labourer James and Mary Ford.*

Eskimo	**Eskimo Skaggs**, born Kentucky, *c.*1894 (Iron Hill, Kentucky, 1910 US census)
Euel	**Euel Hurt**, born Texas, 1899 (Comanche, Texas, 1900 US census)
Eunuch	**Eunuch Evans**, born Carmarthen, 1851
	Eunuch Trusty, born Illinois, *c.*1834 (Chicksaw, Iowa, 1860 US census)
Euphemia	**Euphemia Twat**, baptized Walls, Shetland, 1800. *There were forty-eight Twats in Orkney and Shetland at the time of the 1841 Scotland census. In this same year, in his poem Pippa Passes, Robert Browning included the line 'Cowls and twats', later naively explaining to the editor of the Oxford English Dictionary that he thought a 'twat' was a kind of hood worn by nuns.*
Ever	**Ever Green**, born Lexden, Essex, 1847
Everhard	**Everhard Dick**, born Germany, 28 December 1903 (23 October 1931 application for US naturalization)
Excellent	**Excellent Easter**, born 3 January 1899; died Meridian, Mississippi, USA, January 1971
Extravaganza	**Extravaganza Muriel M. Tomkyns-Grafton**, born Ulverston, Lancashire, 1871
Faintnot	**Faintnot Isaday Bourne**, born Rye, Sussex, 1878
	Faint-not Wood, married William Clarke, Laughton, Sussex, 24 December 1618
Fairest	**Fairest Price**, born North Carolina, *c.*1904 (Duncan, North Carolina, 1910 US census)

Fairy	**Fairy Light** (male), born Tennessee, c.1896 (Dyer, Tennessee, 1910 US census)
	Fairy Wingo, born 5 March 1912; died Dallas, Texas, USA, 1 October 2001
Famous	**Famous Stubblefield**, born 22 February 1903; died Chicago, Illinois, USA, 5 January 1986
Fan	**Fan Dancer**, born Amersham, Buckinghamshire, 1844
Fang	**Fang Smith**, born Hopesay, Shropshire, c.1848 (Woolston, Shropshire, 1851 census)
Fare-well	**Fare-well Sykes**, born Honley, Yorkshire, 1842. *One of the four sons of Sydney and Betty Sykes, Fare-well – who drowned in 1865 – was the brother of Live-well, Do-well and Die-well Sykes.*
Fear	**Fear Brewster**, born Scrooby, Nottinghamshire, c.1586. *Fear and her siblings Patience, Love and Wrestling were among the 'Pilgrim Fathers' who emigrated to America in 1620 aboard the Mayflower. She died in Massachusetts on 12 December 1634. US President Zachary Taylor was a descendant of Fear. The Little Women author, Louisa May Alcott, the singer Bing Crosby and the actress Katharine Hepburn were all Brewster descendants.*
Felia	**Felia Ball**, born North Carolina, c.1880 (Leicester, South Carolina, 1910 US census)
Ferris	**Ferris Wheeler**, born Melksham, Wiltshire, 1860. *He pre-dates the invention of the Ferris wheel (named after its inventor George Washington Gale Ferris) by thirty-three years.*

Festus	**Festus Flipper**, born 15 November 1906; died Savannah, Georgia, USA, 1 November 1996. *His son (1933–92) was also called Festus Flipper.*
Final	**Final Edwin Preston**, born Market Bosworth, Leicestershire, 1892. *Final was, his parents hoped, the last-born of the six children of Lot and Amy Preston.*
Finest	**Finest Fanny**, married Berrie Vista, New Madrid, Missouri, USA, 18 January 1911
Finis	**Finis London**, born Barking, Essex, *c.*1890 (Barking, 1891 census). *Finis ('the end') was apparently the last of the seven children of Alfred and Mary London.*
First-borne and Sadness	**First-borne and Sadness Luffe** (female twins), baptized Aylesbury, Buckinghamshire, 2 September 1656
Fishel	**Fishel Finger**, born Austria, *c.*1861 (Brooklyn, New York, 1930 US census)
Flamina	**Flamina Arsole**, born Lucca, Italy, 6 October 1730
Flappy	**Flappy Downs**, died Daviess [*sic*], Kentucky, USA, 8 February 1994
Flipper	**Flipper Butts**, born 8 February 1919; died Philadelphia, Pennsylvania, USA, November 1975
Fleno	**Fleno Bobo**, born 15 February 1912; died Mississippi, USA, 29 August 1990
Flint	**Flint Stone**, born 15 February 1873; died Arkansas, USA, November 1964
Floppy	**Floppy Pryor**, died Ashton-under-Lyne, Lancashire, 1885
Florist	**Florist Woofter**, born 31 July 1906; died Buckhannon, West Virginia, USA, April 1978

Fly-fornication	**Fly-fornication Andrewes**, baptized Waldron, Sussex, 17 December 1609. *'Bastard son of Catren Andrewes.'*
Free	**Free Love** (female), born Ohio, c.1848 (Liberty, Ohio, 1860 US census)
Free-gift and Fear-not	**Free-gift and Fear-not Lulham** (male twins), baptized Warbleton, Sussex, 12 October 1589
Freelove	**Freelove Noad**, born Melksham, Wiltshire, 1851
Frisby	**Frisby Lightfoot**, born Luton, Bedfordshire, 1873
Frisky	**Frisky Outlaw**, born Georgia, c.1908 (Emanuel, Georgia, 1910 US census)
Fu	**Fu King**, born c.1880; passenger on *Kiyo Maru*, Coronel, Chile–Honolulu, Hawaii, arrived 18 November 1915
Funny	**Funny Sunny Blackshire**, born Louisiana, USA, 23 March 1883; died Carthage, Texas, 29 February 1956
Gassy	**Gassy Pope**, born South Carolina, c.1888 (Charleston, South Carolina, 1920 US census)
Gayman	**Gayman Rackstraw**, married Wandsworth, London, 1899
Genius	**Genius Pickles**, born Wilsden, Yorkshire, c.1855 (Wilsden, 1861 census)

Giant	**Giant Butler**, born 7 August 1908; died Palm Beach, Florida, USA, 3 June 2002
Ginger	**Ginger Ball**, born Ohio, c.1840 (Scioto, Ohio, 1870 US census)
	Ginger Bush, born Pemberton Township, Burlington, New Jersey, USA, 12 July 1861
Globelle	**Globelle W. E. S. Puxley** (male), born Catworth, Huntingdonshire, c.1877 (Kessingland, Suffolk, 1891 census)
Glorious	**Glorious Smith**, born 22 February 1926; died Houston, Texas, USA, 16 March 2003
Gnome	**Gnome Burgess**, born 29 May 1906; died Fort Wayne, Indiana, USA, 30 July 1995
Goblin	**Goblin Reeves**, born Orsett, Essex, 1848
Gobo	**Gobo Fangs**, born Africa, c.1850 (Grantsville City, Utah, 1880 US census)
God-help	**God-help Cooper**, baptized Weybridge, Surrey, 12 June 1628
Golden	**Golden Balls**, baptized Aylsham, Norfolk, 26 September 1813. *His son was also called Golden Balls.*
	Golden Showers, born Arkansas, c.1901 (Prairie, Arkansas, 1920 US census)
Goldie	**Goldie Shower**, born Virginia, c.1902 (Baltimore, Maryland, 1920 US census)
Gonad	**Gonad Green**, born c.1850 (Portland, New York, 1930 US census)
Good	**Good Evans**, born North Carolina, date unknown (Barton Creek, North Carolina, 1900 US census)
Gooden	**Gooden Young**, born Virginia, c.1854 (Clarksville, Virginia, 1910 US census)

Goodluck	**Goodluck Buzagh**, born Middlesex, c.1799 (Lambeth, London, 1851 census)
Goolsby	**Goolsby Scroggins**, born 27 January 1900; died St Louis, Missouri, USA, December 1971
Gracious	**Gracious Lear**, married Ann Clark, Motcombe, Dorset, 30 November 1779
Great	**Great Scott**, born South Carolina, c.1835 (Webster, Georgia, 1870 US census)
Green	**Green Salad**, born Texas, c.1854 (Navarro, Texas, 1880 US census)
Grenade	**Grenade Parson**, born 18 February 1910; died Detroit, Michigan, USA, July 1989
Grimwood	**Grimwood Death**, born c.1810; died Hartismere, Suffolk, 1884. *Several generations of boys in the family were given the name Grimwood Death.*
Gulag	**Gulag Leet**, born North Dakota, 1894 (Freshwater, North Dakota, 1900 US census)
Gusty	**Gusty Sandbag**, born c.1853; died Thornbury, Gloucestershire, 1902
Gypsy	**Gypsy Fish**, born 20 March 1909; died Los Angeles, California, USA, March 1972
Hairy	**Hairy Head**, born Dover, Kent, c.1878 (Dover 1891 census)
	Hairy Mann, married Dover, Kent, 1894
	Hairy Percy Muckley, born Kings Norton, Staffordshire, 1891
Halloween	**Halloween Hummer**, born Indiana, USA, 31 October 1891; died Dunkirk, Indiana, June 1972
Handy	**Handy Mann**, died Croydon, Surrey, 1860

Hansome	**Hansome** [*sic*] **Mann**, born 3 April 1911; died Calhoun, Georgia, USA, 12 August 2001
Hap	**Hap Hazard**, born Illinois, USA, 22 August 1924; died Los Angeles, California, 1 August 1979
Happy	**Happy Balls**, born Blything, Suffolk, 1878
	Happy Fish, died Wangford, Suffolk, 1837
Harmonius [*sic*]	**Harmonius Purity**, born 1 January 1900; died New York, USA, April 1979
Harmony	**Harmony Titus**, born New York, *c*.1828 (Marshall, New York, 1880 US census)
Hashish	**Hashish Moran**, born *c*.1893 (British Army World War I service records)
Hate Evil	**Hate Evil Nutter**, born England 1603; died Dover, New Hampshire, America, 28 June 1675
Helium	**Helium McKinney**, born Mississippi, *c*.1875 (Monroe, Arkansas, 1920 US census)
Heman	**Heman Strong**, died Crow Wing, Minnesota, USA, 13 January 1951
Hepzibah	**Hepzibah Bonker**, born *c*.1826 (Barton Seagrave, Northamptonshire, 1841 census)
High	**High Price**, married Presteigne, Herefordshire, 1861
	High Rockett, married Bridport, Dorset, 1856
Homo	**Homo Jones**, born Cardigan, 1877
Hoorah	**Hoorah Dow**, born *c*.1896 (Woonsocket, South Dakota, 1930 US census)
Huga	**Huga Bottome**, baptized St Margaret's, Leicester, 10 March 1615

Humiliation	**Humiliation Cook**, died Ipswich, Suffolk, 1848
	Humiliation Hinde, married Elizabeth Phillips, St Peter upon Cornhill, London, 24 January 1629
Hyman	**Hyman Finger**, married Mile End, London, 1905
Iceberg	**Iceberg Cumming**, born Georgia, *c.*1820 (Louisville, Alabama, 1880 US census)
Icicle	**Icicle Ashmore**, born Georgia, *c.*1865 (Liberty, Georgia, 1870 US census)
Increase	**Increase Mather**, born Dorchester, Massachusetts, America, 21 June 1629; died Boston, Massachusetts, 23 August 1723. *Increase Mather was a Puritan clergyman, best known for his involvement in the trials of people claimed to be witches in Salem, Massachusetts, in 1692, which resulted in nineteen of them being hanged.*
Increased	**Increased Collins**, born Brightling, Sussex, 30 March 1604. *She was the sister of Changed Collins.*

Indiana	**Indiana Kettle**, born Dudley, Staffordshire, 1854
Infinity	**Infinity Hubbard**, born Georgia, *c*.1839 (Tipah, Mississippi, 1850 US census)
Ingenious	**Ingenious Sylvester**, born Massachusetts, *c*.1816 (Charlestown, Massachusetts, 1850 US census)
Intercydonia	**Intercydonia M. Ball**, married James Jarvis, Wolstanton, Staffordshire, 1912
Iron	**Iron Bum Kelly**, born *c*.1883 (Nevada, 1904 US Indian census)
Isuck	**Isuck Chandler**, born Surrey, *c*.1840 (Carshalton, Surrey, 1841 census)
	Isuck Gibbons, born Georgia, *c*.1875 (Savannah, Georgia, 1880 US census)
	Isuck Gordon, born Alabama, *c*.1867 (Alabama, 1870 US census)
Janita	**Janita Tit**, born Netherlands, *c*.1872; passenger on *Westernland*, Antwerp, Belgium–New York, USA, arrived 22 February 1932
Job-rakt-out-of-the-asshes [*sic*]	**Job-rakt-out-of-the-asshes**, baptized St Helen, Bishopsgate, London, 1 September 1611
Jolly	**Jolly Joy**, born Texas, *c*.1904 (Sulphur Springs, Texas, 1910 US census)
Joy-in-sorrow	**Joy-in-sorrow Godman**, married Joseph Baysie, All Saints, Lewes, Sussex, 20 May 1614
Juggler	**Juggler Woodhouse**, married Runcorn, Cheshire, 1884

Juggy	**Juggy Williams** (female), married John Price, Almeley, Herefordshire, 24 May 1792
Jugs	**Jugs Ferner**, born Scotland, *c.*1896 (East Ham, Essex, 1901 census)
	Jugs Lykken, born Russia, *c.*1864; passenger on *Arabic*, Liverpool, England–New York, USA, arrived 30 April 1888
Juicy	**Juicy Jones**, born Florida, 1861 (Robinson, Florida, 1900 US census)
Jupiter	**Jupiter Battle**, born 24 November 1899; died Detroit, Michigan, USA, May 1965
Justa	**Justa Crook**, born London, *c.*1855 (Mile End, London, 1901 census)
Kickback	**Kickback Lockhart**, born Alabama, *c.*1895 (Jernigan, Alabama, 1910 US census)
Klingon	**Klingon Potts**, born Pennsylvania, *c.*1853 (Cecil, Maryland, 1880 US census)
Kraken	**Kraken Papen**, born Germany, *c.*1845 (Ridott, Illinois, 1850 US census)
Labour	**Labour Hendershot**, born Indiana, *c.*1855 (Berkeley, California, 1930 US census)
Ladie	**Ladie Gagapley**, born Wisconsin, *c.*1896 (Green Bay, Wisconsin, 1910 US census)
Lament	**Lament Bible**, married Nicholas Hussher, Ticehurst, Sussex, 9 September 1640
Lamentation	**Lamentation Brazille**, married David Loring, Hancock, Georgia, USA, 25 January 1838
	Lamentation Bullivant, born Spilsby, Lincolnshire, 1841
Larceny	**Larceny Fooks**, born Virginia, *c.*1890 (Somerset, Maryland, 1920 US census)

Large	**Large Bee**, born Nottinghamshire, *c*.1829 (Nottingham, 1891 census). *His son was also called Large Bee.*
Last	**Last Child**, born Runham, Norfolk, *c*.1866 (Great Yarmouth, Norfolk, 1871 census). *He was not in fact the last child of Henry and Susanna Child, but the fifth of six.*
	Last First, born Florida, USA, 12 May 1907; died Winter Haven, Florida, 22 April 1982
Leaky	**Leaky Broom**, born Mississippi, *c*.1885 (Marion, Mississippi, 1920 US census)
Lean	**Lean Bacon**, born Pennsylvania, *c*.1876 (Tioga, Pennsylvania, 1910 US census)
Leptimus	**Leptimus Pants**, born Middlesbrough, Yorkshire, *c*.1872 (Oldham, Lancashire, 1911 census)
Leviathan	**Leviathan Buttress**, born Stevenage, Hertfordshire, *c*.1853 (Bartlow, Cambridgeshire, 1881 census)
Leyline	**Leyline Smith**, born Georgia, *c*.1908 (Turner, Georgia, 1910 US census)
Lezza	**Lezza Scragg**, born Burslem, Staffordshire, *c*.1860 (Burslem, 1861 census)
Liberal	**Liberal Reform Derby**, born Tendring, Essex, 1850
Licka	**Licka Licka**, born France 1903; passenger on *La Bretagne*, Le Havre, France–New York, USA, arrived 14 May 1906
Long	**Long Cock**, born Channel Islands, *c*.1853 (Alameda, California, 1910 US census)
	Long Dick, born California, *c*.1865 (Alpine, California, 1910 US census)
	Long Dong, born China, *c*.1887 (Spokane, Washington, 1930 US census)

Lord	**Lord Baron**, born Haslingden, Lancashire, 1842
Low	**Low Fat**, married Cardiff, Glamorgan, 1905
	Low Fee, married Chorlton, Cheshire, 1908
	Low Sum, died Cardiff, Glamorgan, 1909
Lunabella	**Lunabella S. Heagorty**, born Cork, Ireland, c.1870 (Limehouse, London, 1881 census). *She was the daughter of Lunabella c. Heagorty.*
Lurid	**Lurid Caldwell**, born Argyll, c.1857 (Greenock, Renfrewshire, 1871 Scotland census)
Lurking	**Lurking Crabb**, born Gosfield, Essex, c.1780 (West Hanningfield, Essex, 1861 census)
Lustrous	**Lustrous Luke Smith**, married Ipswich, Suffolk, 1858
Luther	**Luther Denmark Longbottom**, born Silsden, Yorkshire, c.1848 (Silsden, 1881 census)
Magic	**Magic Enchantress Creamer**, born 23 February 1974; died California, USA, 3 December 2007
Magnify	**Magnify Beard**, baptized Warbleton, Sussex, 17 September 1587
Major	**Major Belcher**, born 1 May 1898; died Big Rock, Buchanan, Virginia, USA, May 1984
	Major Leak, died Spalding, Lincolnshire, 1855
	Major Major, born Islington, London, 1871
	Major Minor, born Arkansas, c.1882 (Hot Springs, Arkansas, 1910 US census)

Mammary	**Mammary Label**, born New Brunswick, 1898 (New Brunswick, 1911 Canada census)
Marathon	**Marathon Mary Judge**, born 1909; died Chiltern, Buckinghamshire, 1999
Marijuana	**Marijuana Archuleta**, died El Paso, Texas, USA, 10 February 1913
Marquis	**Marquis Baron**, born Burnley, Lancashire, 1880
	Marquis Marquis F. Puschart, married St Saviour, London, 1892
Mars and Venus	**Mars and Venus Neptune** (twins), born Wyoming, USA, 16 March 1897
Master	**Master Bates**, born Pulaski, Kentucky, USA, 16 December 1859
Mastin	**Mastin Bates**, born London, c.1866 (Scredington, Lincolnshire, 1881 census)
Maximum	**Maximum Aid**, born France, c.1821 (New Lexington, Ohio, 1870 US census)
Maximus	**Maximus Curd**, born Kentucky, c.1859 (Calloway, Kentucky, 1860 US census)
Meditation	**Meditation Gay**, born Lambeth, London, 1847
Medium	**Medium Light**, died Henley, Oxfordshire, 1849
Memory	**Memory Lane**, born Alabama, c.1875 (Limestone, Alabama, 1880 US census)
Mephibosheth	**Mephibosheth Capstack**, born Halifax, Yorkshire, 1869 (Northowram, Yorkshire, 1871 census)
Mercye	**Mercye Bike**, baptized Thornhill by Dewsbury, Yorkshire, 9 February 1651

Merkin	**Merkin King**, born Nassington, Northamptonshire, *c.*1837 (Nassington, 1871 census). *A merkin is a pubic wig worn by prostitutes. The word first appeared in print in English in 1617.*
Merrie	**Merrie Tart Knox**, born Fifeshire, *c.*1770 (St Ninians, Stirlingshire, 1851 Scotland census)
Messy	**Messy Licker** (female), born Chorley, Lancashire, *c.*1803 (Manchester, 1861 census)
Meteor	**Meteor Lafleur**, born 6 October 1912; died Kinder, Texas, USA, 7 January 1990
Methuselah	**Methuselah Shonk**, born *c.*1836; died Romford, Essex, 1902
Minnehaha/ Minniehaha	**Minnehaha Clements**, born Wandsworth, London, 1874
	Minniehaha Smith, born Gravesend, Kent, no date recorded (Gravesend, 1881 census)
Minor	**Minor Major**, born Missouri, *c.*1898 (Jackson, Missouri, 1910 US census)
Minty	**Minty Badger**, married Southam, Warwickshire, 1866
Moist	**Moist Laforest**, born Canada, 1850 (Providence, Rhode Island, 1900 US census). *His son was also called Moist Laforest.*

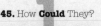

Mojo	**Mojo Lampe**, born 29 November 1912; died Everett, Washington, USA, January 1986
Mont	**Mont Blanc**, born c.1806; died Huddersfield, Yorkshire, 1881
More-fruit	**More-fruit Fenner**, baptized Cranbrook, Kent, 22 December 1583. *Dudley Fenner (c.1558–1587), preacher of Romford, Essex, was accused of baptizing children with such names as Joy-again and From-above, but defended himself by pointing out that he had given his own daughters the names More-fruit, Faint-not and Dust.*
	More-fruit Stone, baptized Alfriston, Sussex, 6 June 1587. *The father of Zealous Stone.*
Morning	**Morning Dew**, born Altrincham, Cheshire, 1871
Mossie	**Mossie Husbands**, born 9 April 1911; died Gadsden, Florida, USA, 30 June 1971
Munch	**Munch Cox** (female), born Devon, c.1791 (Ottery St Mary, Devon, 1841 census)
Murder	**Murder John Smith**, born St George Hanover Square, London, 1878
My	**My Space**, born Idaho, c.1903 (Pierce, Idaho, 1910 US census)
Myball	**Myball Barton**, born Lancashire, c.1816 (Preston, Lancashire, 1841 census)
Myboob	**Myboob Bux**, born Kensington, London, 1859
Mydick	**Mydick Buck**, died Crawfordsville, Indiana, USA, 12 September 1912
Mystic	**Mystic Smith**, born South Stoneham, Hampshire, 1855
Naughty	**Naughty Burkhammer**, born 1894; died Weston, West Virginia, USA, 14 January 1939

Nebuchadnezzar	**Nebuchadnezzar Smith**, born Hollingbourne, Kent, 1882
Nemesis	**Nemesis Conrad**, born Strand, London, 1878
Never	**Never Fail**, born Texas, USA, 30 June 1906; died Tulsa, Oklahoma, June 1973
	Never Gamble, born South Carolina, c.1887 (Leesburg, Florida, 1930 US census)
	Never Wait, born Manchester, Lancashire, c.1834 (Warrington, Lancashire, 1891 census)
Nobrian	**Nobrian Jones**, born c.1899; passenger on *Stratheden*, Brisbane, Australia–Liverpool, UK, arrived 18 July 1940. *It is assumed that his first name was correctly recorded as a unique example of 'Nobrian' and not a dyslexic version of 'Nobrain'.*
No-merit	**No-merit Vynall**, baptized Warbleton, Sussex, 28 September 1589
No More	**No More Durrant**, born Risbridge, Suffolk, 1899
Nosy	**Nosy Allen**, born St Clement, Oxford, c.1883 (St Clement, 1891 census)
Not Wanted	**Not Wanted Carroll**, born Ohio, 1850 (Brush Creek, Ohio, 1850 US census). *Not Wanted was the newborn ninth child of Enoch and Elizabeth Carroll.*
	Not Wanted James Colvill, born (and died) Lambeth, London, 1861
Notwithstanding	**Notwithstanding Griswold**, born Durham, Connecticut, America, 16 April 1764
Oakley	**Oakley Homer**, born West Virginia, c.1859 (Gallipolis, Ohio, 1930 US census)

Ocean	**Ocean Rolls**, born Cookham, Berkshire, 1869
Ocellous	**Ocellous Hardwick**, born 17 July 1893; died Adair, Kentucky, USA, 21 October 1984
Ofelia	**Ofelia Arce**, baptized La Merced, Chachapoyas, Peru, 15 March 1890
	Ofelia Comes, born Spain, c.1894; passenger on *Antonio Lopez*, Havana, Cuba–New York, USA, arrived 6 March 1924
Offspring	**Offspring Jeeves**, married Sophia Dear, Arlesey, Bedfordshire, 21 January 1854. *'Offspring' is occasionally encountered where a newborn baby is recorded before it has been named, but it appears to have been used as a first name among several generations of the Jeeves, Dear and Webb families of Arlesey, the location of a well-known lunatic asylum.*
Okla	**Okla Homer Watts**, born South Carolina, USA, 29 December 1912; died Whiteville, South Carolina, 23 June 1968
Old	**Old Book Thomspilie**, born Congleton, Cheshire, c.1863 (Hulme, Lancashire, 1871 census)
Oldest	**Oldest Young**, born Alabama, c.1907 (Jefferson, Alabama, 1920 US census)
Onabelle	**Onabelle Shopbell**, born 1 February 1886; died Battle Creek, Michigan, USA, November 1968
One Too Many	**One Too Many Gouldstone**, born West Ham, Essex, 1870
Ono	**Ono Prescott**, born Wigan, Lancashire, 1887
Oofty	**Oofty Goofty Bowman**, married Fannie Edwards, St Joseph, Indiana, USA, 9 May 1913

Opportune	**Opportune Ganwit**, born France, *c*.1842 (Shirburn, Oxfordshire, 1871 census)
Opportunity	**Opportunity Hopper**, married Thomas Lunt, Salem, Massachusetts, USA, 22 December 1680
Optimus	**Optimus Mason**, died Sheffield, Yorkshire, 1930
Organ	**Organ B. Long**, married Jennie Pruett, Dekalb, Alabama, USA, 22 December 1893
Original	**Original Bottom**, born Lockwood, Yorkshire, 1846
	Original Bugg, born Lincoln, 1907
Orion	**Orion Belt**, born 23 March 1922; died New Windsor, Maryland, USA, 6 March 2006
	Orion Over Price, born *c*.1812 (Merthyr Tydfil, Glamorgan, 1841 Wales census)
Oxygen	**Oxygen Smith**, born 11 August 1937; died New York, USA, 16 May 2008
Peaceable	**Peaceable Sherwood**, baptized Thurlaston, Leicestershire, 15 January 1597. *He emigrated to America and was recorded as living in Virginia in 1623.*
Peculiar	**Peculiar Cannon**, born Claypole, Lincolnshire, *c*.1876 (Hawton, Nottinghamshire, 1881 census)
	Peculiar Lay (female), born *c*.1820 (Kit Carson, Colorado, 1870 US census)
	Peculiar Stringer, born *c*.1803; died Wolverhampton, Staffordshire, 1882
Peinus	**Peinus Anus** (male), born New York, *c*.1855 (New York; 1860 US census)
Perfect	**Perfect Perfect**, born Chatham, Kent, *c*.1887 (Chatham, 1891 census)

Perpetual	**Perpetual Brown**, born 15 July 1938; died Festus, Missouri, USA, 19 April 2009
Perpugilliam	**Perpugilliam Smith**, born West Bromwich, Staffordshire, 1847
Perseverance	**Perseverance Green**, born Amsterdam, Netherlands, c.1603; arrived Charlestown, Massachusetts, America, 1632
	Perseverance Smith, born Fulham, London, 1876
Pharoah	**Pharoah Stingemore**, born Axbridge, Somerset, 1875
Phelía	**Phelia Legg**, born Gloucestershire, c.1826 (Kempsford, Gloucestershire, 1841 census)
Philadelphia	**Philadelphia Bunnyface**, Laneast, Cornwall (will, 1722). *The inclusion of this name among those published by the Cornwall Record Office in its list of 'Silly Names' upset some people called Boniface, who believed the name to be a corruption of theirs.*
Philetus	**Philetus Fish**, born Uxbridge, Middlesex, 1844
Phosphorus	**Phosphorus Stone**, married Stepney, London, 1866
Phuk	**Phuk Thong**, born 10 February 1921; died Des Moines, Iowa, USA, 18 April 1996
Phuker	**Phuker William**, born Staffordshire, c.1791 (Betley, Staffordshire, 1841 census)
Pincus	**Pincus Elephant**, born Russia, c.1886 (New York, 1910 US census)
Pink	**Pink Cock** (male), born Texas, c.1870 (Harrison, Texas, 1880 US census)

THIS IS WHAT I DO TO FATHER!

Pinkie/ Pinkey/ Pinky	**Pinkey Penis** (female), born Mississippi, *c.*1870 (Tate, Mississippi, 1900 US census)
	Pinkie Balls, died Milam, Texas, USA, 31 December 1917
	Pinkie Beaver, born *c.*1897 (Unicoi, Tennessee, 1930 US census)
	Pinky Bottoms, born Missouri, 1887 (Pacific City, Missouri, 1900 US census)
Pinkus	**Pinkus Gash**, born Russia, *c.*1888 (Spitalfields, London, 1891 census). *Pinkus was the son of Fanny and Isaac Gash.*
Pirate	**Pirate Black**, born 3 August 1922; died San Francisco, California, USA, 2 April 2006
	Pirate King, born Missouri, *c.*1835 (Richmond, Missouri, 1880 US census)
Planet	**Planet Jones**, born Breconshire, *c.*1839 (Lower Ystradgynlais, 1841 Wales census)

Platinum	**Platinum Caldwell**, born Washington, c.1891 (Spokane, Washington, 1920 US census)
Plato	**Plato Smith**, born Blything, Suffolk, 1880
Pleasant	**Pleasant Spanks**, born c.1901 (Vernon, Louisiana, 1930 US census)
Plunger	**Plunger Sharpe**, born Georgia, USA, 19 November 1897
Pluto	**Pluto Oulton**, born Manchester, Lancashire, 1871
Poke	**Poke Sharpley**, born Macclesfield, Cheshire, c.1823 (Macclesfield, 1891 census)
Pope	**Pope Smyrk**, married Brighton, East Sussex, 1907
Postal	**Postal Smalls**, born 9 October 1919; died Huger, South Carolina, USA, 11 December 2008
Posthumous	**Posthumous Mince**, died Greenwich, Kent, 1839
Preserved	**Preserved Emms**, died St Nicholas, Yarmouth, 17 November 1712
	Preserved Fish, born Portsmouth, Rhode Island, America, 16 March 1677; died Portsmouth, 15 July 1744. *There were several people called Preserved Fish in America – another (born 14 July 1766; died 23 July 1846) was a well-known merchant in New York.*
	Preserved McDonald, born Elgin, Moray, c.1810 (Elgin, 1851 Scotland census)
	Preserved Moose, resident of Crawford County, Arkansas, USA (tax list, 1836)
	Preserved Pears, resident of Rehoboth, Massachusetts (1800 US census)

President	**President Goggins**, born 3 March 1900; died Anniston, Alabama, USA, February 1981
	President Percy Smith, born Poplar, London, 1882
Prima	**Prima Donna Charlotte Mildren**, baptized St Mawes, Cornwall, 11 April 1870
Primitive	**Primitive Dorbat**, born 28 June 1928; died Bridgeport, Connecticut, USA, 20 May 2003
Prince	**Prince Charles Whales**, born Mitford, Norfolk, 1899
	Prince Cock (female), born Texas, *c.*1873 (Weatherford, Texas, 1880 US census)
Princess	**Princess Gladys Glastonbury**, born Keynsham, Somerset, 1902
Prod	**Prod Busby**, born Sussex, *c.*1816 (Midhurst, Sussex, 1841 census)
Professor	**Professor Hydropath Mort**, born Birmingham, Warwickshire, 1868. *'Professor' was his first name, not his academic title.*
Pubecca	**Pubecca Hare**, born Kent, *c.*1831 (Minster, Kent, 1841 census)
Purple	**Purple Starkweather**, born Connecticut, *c.*1781 (Milton, Vermont, 1850 US census)
Queen	**Queen Prince**, died Chester, Cheshire, 1894
	Queen Victoria, born *c.*1840 (Edmonton, Middlesex, 1851 census)
	Queen Victoria Smith, born Rochford, Essex, 1901
Question	**Question James**, born Williton, Somerset, 1880

Quick	**Quick French**, died Eastbourne, Sussex, 1881
Rapeme	**Rapeme Obabachïan**, mother of Joseph Houssepian, married Zeda Maxudian, marriage banns, Paris, France, 31 January 1897
Reader	**Reader Book**, born Alabama, 1899 (Fox Creek, Alabama, 1900 US census)
Reality	**Reality Newton**, born Tennessee, 1891 (Logan Oklahoma, 1900 US census)
Redeemed	**Redeemed Compton**, born Battle, Sussex, 1588
Rehab	**Rehab Allwright**, born Cholsey, Oxfordshire, c.1843 (Cholsey, 1851 census). *Rehab's siblings included Parfet and Quiet.*
Rejoice	**Rejoice Wratten**, baptized Warbleton, Sussex, 18 October 1679
Remarkable	**Remarkable Cheney**, born Nevada, c.1870 (Carson City, Nevada, 1870 US census)
Repent	**Repent Champney**, baptized Warbleton, Sussex, 14 August 1608. *'A bastard.'*
Repentance	**Repentance Wrath**, baptized Elham, Kent, 26 March 1612
Replenish	**Replenish French**, baptized Warbleton, Sussex, 13 May 1660
Restored	**Restored Weekes**, married Constant Sumar, Chiddingly, Sussex, 27 August 1618
Reverend	**Reverend James Ball**, born Doncaster, Yorkshire, 1878. *'Reverend' was his first name.*
Rich	**Rich Cousins**, died Epping, Essex, 1851
	Rich Lathers, born South Carolina, c.1870 (Fruit Cove, Florida, 1910 US census)

Risky	**Risky Walker**, born Harrington, Cumberland, *c.*1880 (Parton, Cumberland, 1880 census)
Risque	**Risque Booth**, born Stockport, Cheshire, 1909
River	**River Jordan**, baptized English Bicknor, Gloucestershire, 16 November 1766
Rock	**Rock Star**, born Italy, 1886 (Jackson, Missouri, 1900 US census)
Rocket	**Rocket Hodgson**, born Brotherton, Yorkshire, *c.*1878 (Brotherton, 1881 census)
Rockus	**Rockus Roll**, born USA, *c.*1909 (Hettinger, North Dakota, 1910 US census)
Rocky	**Rocky Mountain**, born Alameda, California, USA, 22 October 1922; died Paradise, California, 25 October 2002
Rolla	**Rolla Long**, born Texas, *c.*1905 (Tulare, California, 1910 US census)
Rollin	**Rollin Stone**, born 19 May 1896; died Ringgold, Georgia, USA, 31 May 1987
Rotunda	**Rotunda Ross**, born North Carolina, *c.*1858 (Hancock, Illinois, 1870 US census)
Safe-on-high	**Safe-on-high Hopkinson**, baptized Salehurst, Sussex, 28 February 1591
Safety	**Safety First**, born Pennsylvania, USA, 23 March 1894; died Seal Beach, Orange, California, 20 April 1985. *His sister June First was born in Pennsylvania in c.1905.*
Saint	**Saint Bugg**, died Bourne, Lincolnshire, 1840
Santa	**Santa Claus**, born 10 June 1930; died Reidsville, North Carolina, USA, 10 September 2008

Satisfy	**Satisfy Sparkes**, married John Lewis, Delaware, USA, 7 February 1809
Science	**Science Gore**, born Liverpool, Lancashire, *c*.1869 (Bevington, Lancashire, 1871 census)
Seaflower	**Seaflower Rolls**, born Cookham, Berkshire, 1875. *Seaflower was the sister of Benbow, Bluebell, Daisy, May, Ocean and Snowdrop Rolls.*
Seldom	**Seldom Wright** (male), born Mississippi, *c*.1880 (Memphis, Tennessee, 1910 US census)
Semion	**Semion Staines** (male), born Maldon, Essex, *c*.1863 (Maldon, 1871 census)
Sensitive	**Sensitive Redhead** (female), born Bridlington, Yorkshire, 1873
Septuagesima	**Septuagesima Bone Bone**, born Walsingham, Norfolk, 1875
Serious	**Serious Funny**, born South Carolina, *c*.1872 (Georgetown, South Carolina, 1930 US census)
Sexa	**Sexa Beard**, born Axbridge, Somerset, 1855
Sexbus	**Sexbus Dyball**, born Ludlow, Shropshire, *c*.1832; died Reigate, Surrey, 1898
Sexey	**Sexey Jane Smith**, born *c*.1842; died Amesbury, Wiltshire, 1898
Sexy	**Sexy Cook**, died Bedminster, Somerset, 1848
Shaft	**Shaft Nest**, born Tennessee, *c*.1900 (Madison, Tennessee, 1930 US census)
Shavette	**Shavette Hopkins**, died Harris, Texas, USA, 9 February 1991

Shay	**Shay King**, born 19 October 1947; died Charleston, South Carolina, USA, May 1981
Shepherd	**Shepherd Pyes**, born North Dakota, USA, 15 September 1889 (Grand Forks, North Dakota, World War I draft registration)
Shepherdess	**Shepherdess Jane Backhoffner**, born St Marylebone, London, 1845 (St Marylebone, 1851 census). *Shepherdess was the daughter of George H. Backhoffner, Professor of Chemistry and Natural Philosophy and Registrar of Births and Deaths – so one would think he might have known better than to give his daughter a silly name...*
Sidwella	**Sidwella Splat**, married William Small, Chagford, Devon, 21 June 1613
Silence	**Silence Bacon**, born South Normanton, Derbyshire, c.1822 (South Normanton, 1871 census)
	Silence Bottom, married Thomas Mason, Chesterfield, Derbyshire, 26 October 1735
Silent	**Silent Knight**, baptized Dorchester, Dorset, 24 December 1607
Silly	**Silly Price**, born Sheffield, Yorkshire, c.1855 (Sheffield, 1891 census)
Sin-deny	**Sin-deny Hely**, married William Swane, Burwash, Sussex, 4 September 1621

Sinderella [*sic*]	**Sinderella Small**, born Cornwall, *c.*1853 (Newton Abbot, Devon, 1881 census)
Sing	**Sing Song**, died Liverpool, Lancashire, 1847
Singular	**Singular Onion Gallehawk**, born Sheppey, Kent, 1850
Sir	**Sir Dusty Entwistle**, born Bury, Lancashire, *c.*1877 (Bury, 1881 census)
Sirjohn	**Sirjohn Robinson**, baptized Old Church, St Pancras, London, 22 March 1796
Skeleton	**Skeleton D. Popplewell**, born Kentucky, 1868 (Wolf Creek, Kentucky, 1900 US census)
Smiley	**Smiley Badger**, born Napton, Warwickshire, *c.*1888 (Southam, Warwickshire, 1901 census)
Snow	**Snow Shovel Curley**, born Oklahoma, *c.*1890 (Lincoln, Oklahoma, 1900 US census)
Socialist	**Socialist Stewart**, born Massachusetts, 1850 (Braintree, Massachusetts, 1850 US census). *Socialist was the newborn brother of Osceola Stewart.*
Sorry-for-sin	**Sorry-for-sin Coupard**, baptized Warbleton, Sussex, 25 January 1589
Sosthenes	**Sosthenes Sille**, born 4 August 1921; died Schenectady, New York, USA, 16 March 2008
Spanner	**Spanner Bing**, born Northwood, Isle of Wight, *c.*1822 (Newchurch, Hampshire, 1851 census)
Spark	**Spark Spinks**, born Thetford, Norfolk, 1840
Sphinx	**Sphinx Turner**, born 29 May 1913; died Mobile, Alabama, USA, 15 May 1997

Star	**Star Light**, born 12 August 1912; died New York, USA, January 1980
Starlight	**Starlight D. V. Le Garde**, married William H. Jones, Llanrwst, Denbighshire, 1913
Straiton	**Straiton Hard**, born New York, USA, 28 November 1884
Streaker	**Streaker Smith**, born Easington, Durham, 1845
Strongman	**Strongman Fussell**, born Rochester, Kent, c.1821 (Newington, London, 1881 census)
Submarine	**Submarine Miners Banacks**, born Kingston upon Hull, Yorkshire, c.1837 (Kingston upon Hull, 1891 census)
Suca	**Suca Prick**, born Reed, Suffolk, c.1753
Success	**Success Boroughs**, born 1833; died Sumter, South Carolina, USA, 30 November 1921
Sucker	**Sucker Willis**, born North Carolina, c.1896 (Smyrna, North Carolina, 1910 US census)
Sucky	**Sucky Trevithick**, born Cornwall, c.1903 (St Ives, Cornwall, 1841 census)
Sucofa	**Sucofa Johnson**, born Virginia, c.1867 (Spartanburg, South Carolina, 1920 US census)
Sundance	**Sundance Cravat**, born 3 January 1915; died Las Vegas, Nevada, USA, February 1986
Supplement	**Supplement Zepp**, born Germany, 1848 (St Louis, Missouri, 1900 US census)
Surgeon	**Surgeon Kershaw**, born Basford, Nottinghamshire, 1860
Tarzan	**Tarzan Branch**, born 27 February 1922; died Alexandria, Virginia, USA, 24 April 2008

Teepee	**Teepee Hart**, born Texas, 1900 (Waco, Texas, 1900 US census)
Telegraph	**Telegraph Dick**, born c.1844; died Bishop Auckland, Durham, 1877
Temperantia	**Temperantia Google**, baptized Aldborough, Norfolk, 13 August 1598
Temptress	**Temptress Sheba Allen**, born 30 September 1963; died Pasadena, California, USA, 31 May 2009
Time	**Time Of Day**, born Hoo, Kent, 1899
Titus	**Titus Tits**, married Jane Bodet, New York, America, 1726
Toe	**Toe Nail**, born c.1830 (South Dakota, 1897 US Indian census)
Too Many	**Too Many Whitehead**, born North Carolina, 1880 (Swift Creek, North Carolina, 1880 US census). *Too Many was the latest of Allen and Lucinda Whitehead's six children.*
Trannie	**Trannie Percy Hampshire**, born Chertsey, Surrey, c.1897 (Chertsey, 1901 census)
Triffiddus	**Triffiddus Mann**, born Ontario, c.1841 (Carleton, Ontario, 1891 Canada census)
True	**True Blue**, born 17 September 1888; died Lebo, Kansas, USA, February 1972
	True Love, born Newington, London, 1848
Truly	**Truly Carbon**, born Dorking, Surrey, c.1869 (Broadwater Down, Kent, 1901 census)
	Truly Irish, born 28 February 1898; died St Louis, Missouri, USA, December 1984
Ty	**Ty Coon**, born c.1967; died Tacoma, Washington, USA, 21 May 1985

Underdown	**Underdown Knell**, born Maidstone, Kent, 1840
Unique	**Unique Glass**, born Oklahoma, c.1903 (Oklahoma City, 1930 US census)
United	**United States**, born 19 February 1911; died Hopewell, Virginia, USA, 29 February 2000
University	**University Diana Pembrook**, born St Pancras, London, 1898
Uranus	**Uranus Sparks**, born 13 July 1921; married Macon, Alabama, USA, August 1956; died 1 December 1990
	Uranus Wild, born North Carolina, c.1879 (Warm Springs, North Carolina, 1880 US census)
Urban	**Urban Eclipse Wyvill**, born Fulham, London, 1888
Urethra	**Urethra Scoggins**, born Georgia, 1892 (Wrightsville, Georgia, 1900 US census)
Utterly	**Utterly Bowles**, married Mary A. E. Hollier, Melton Mowbray, Leicestershire, 1918
Vanity	**Vanity Quackenbush**, born c.1906 (North Hempstead, New York, 1930 US census)
Velveteen	**Velveteen Sailors**, born 15 April 1927; died Tucker, Georgia, USA, 19 January 2004
Vendetta	**Vendetta Hoover**, born Indiana, c.1906 (Franklin, Ohio, 1920 US census)
Virgin	**Virgin Rackstraw**, died Wycombe, Buckinghamshire, 1896
Viscount	**Viscount Heavican**, born Bury, Lancashire, 1890 (Bury, 1891 census). *'Viscount' was his first name.*

Wallop	**Wallop Brabazon**, married Jane Du Pre, St Marylebone, London, 19 March 1796
Wan	**Wan Kerr**, born Ontario, c.1882 (Bothwell, Ontario, 1891 Canada census)
Wave	**Wave Feather**, born Windsor, Berkshire, c.1825 (Hampton, Middlesex, 1851 census)
Wealthy	**Wealthy Beard**, married Gloucester, 1867
	Wealthy Driver, born Alabama, c.1853 (Young, Texas, 1880 US census)
What	**What Peace**, born Huddersfield, Yorkshire, 1854
Whatnot	**Olive Lily Whatnot Neaves**, baptized St James, Pentonville, London, 5 February 1905
Whatson	**Whatson Gathercole**, born Cornwall, 1889
Wholesome	**Wholesome Bayliss**, born 27 January 1920; died Surrey, 1985
Wiggy	**Wiggy Piggy**, born Virginia, c.1878 (Richmond, Virginia, 1880 US census)
Wighead	**Wighead Spott**, born England, c.1863; passenger on *Germanic*, Liverpool, England–New York, USA, arrived 13 March 1896
Wiki	**Wiki Baldwin**, born Middlesex, c.1839 (Holborn, London, 1841 census)
Wincenty	**Wincenty Bonk**, born 23 July 1892; died Wilmington, Delaware, USA, March 1971
Winter	**Winter Day**, born Romsey, Hampshire, 1845
	Winter Frost, born Kidderminster, Worcestershire, 1859

Wonderland	**Wonderland Potts**, born Missouri, *c.*1888 (Wichita, Kansas, 1920 US census)
Wong	**Wong Kee**, born China, *c.*1874 (aboard ship *Glenlochy*, Middlesbrough, Yorkshire, 1901 census)
Wonky	**Wonky Purdom**, born Hoxton, London, *c.*1879 (Hemel Hempstead, Hertfordshire, 1891 census)
Wood	**Wood Burns**, born Louisiana, *c.*1875 (Union, Louisiana, 1880 US census)
Wooloomooloo	**Wooloomooloo Roscoe**, born Oldham, Lancashire, 1876
Woosh	**Woosh Nook**, born British Columbia, *c.*1849 (Vancouver, British Columbia, 1901 Canada census)
Worthy	**Worthy Extra**, married Malmesbury, Wiltshire, 1865
Wow	**Wow Ashworth**, born Lancashire, *c.*1771 (Blackburn, Lancashire, 1841 census)
Yahoo	**Yahoo Brown**, died Sheslay, British Columbia, Canada, 10 March 1937
York	**York Hunt**, born Georgia, *c.*1845 (Pike, Georgia, 1870 US census). *Like Mike Hunt, York Hunt is one of those 'depends how you say it' names.*
Zaiboon	**Zaiboon McDoom**, born 11 November 1916; died Waltham Forest, London, 2003
Zealous	**Zealous Stone**, baptized Hellingley, Sussex, 8 March 1612
Zebbedee	**Zebbedee Steptoe**, born Virginia, *c.*1909 (Lynchburg, Virginia, 1910 US census)
Zeus	**Zeus Smith**, born Missouri, 1889 (Douglas, Wisconsin, 1900 US census)

Don't Even Think About It

You wouldn't, would you? But there follows an awful warning in the form of those who named their children after private parts and sexual activities. I can also reliably inform you that among America's inhabitants there have been a Legover McCool and a Spunk Beard. One may speculate on whether any of them ever met – it could have been one hell of a party.

Anal	**Anal Cheek**, born Arkansas, c.1905 (Okemah, Oklahoma, 1920 US census)
	Anal Leak, born Canada, 1902; married Mildred Inness, Royal Oak, Wayne, Michigan, USA, 5 August 1923
Analey	**Analey Larking**, died Sevenoaks, Kent, 1843
Anus	**Anus Arslanyan**, born 1917; died Bexley, Kent, 2004
	Anus C. Rapp, born Indiana, 1887 (Chicago, Illinois, 1910 US census)
	Anus Fish, born Iowa, c.1871 (Jefferson Woods, Oklahoma, 1920 US census)
	Anus Hughes, died St Asaph, Denbighshire, 1847
	Anus Lane, born Marylebone, London, 1879
	Anus Price, born Missouri, 1870 (Tavern, Pulaski, Missouri, 1880 US census)
	Anus Ruff, born South Carolina, c.1875 (Heller, Newberry, South Carolina, 1920 US census)

Arse, etc.	**Arse Oats**, born Florida, 1898 (Walton, Florida, 1900 US census)
	Arse Silverhorn, born Wisconsin, 1897 (Jefferson City, Wisconsin, 1900 US census)
	Arseman Whitteron, born Plumpton, Yorkshire, c.1881 (Spofforth, Yorkshire, 1891 census)
	Arsena Titus, born New York, c.1826 (Hamburg, Erie, New York, 1850 US census)
	Arsey Cubbin, born Isle of Man, c.1868 (Braddan, Isle of Man, 1871 Isle of Man census)
	Arshola Roberson, born South Carolina, 1890 (Palmetto, South Carolina, 1900 US census)
	Arsie Bush, died Toombs, Georgia, USA, 11 December 1964
	Arsie Poe, died Fayette, Alabama, USA, 9 April 1946
Balls	**Balls Baxter**, born Depwade, Norfolk, 1854
Bollock	**Bollock Fisher**, born Ohio, 1900 (Cleveland City, Cuyahoga, Ohio, 1900 US census)
	Bollock Trotsky, born Pennsylvania, c.1911 (Northampton, Pennsylvania, 1920 US census)
Boner	**Boner Allgood** (male), born Georgia, c.1903 (Temple, Georgia, 1920 US census)

Bonk	**Bonk Cox**, born Arkansas, c.1904 (Eudora, Arkansas, 1930 US census)
	Bonk Register, born Florida, 1862 (Hamilton, Florida, 1880 US census)
Boob(y)	**Boob Driver**, born Tennessee, c.1898 (Puncheon, Kentucky, 1930 US census)
	Booby Ogle, born Kentucky, 1882 (Buthersville, Kentucky, 1900 US census)
Bottom	**Bottom Lay**, born Mississippi, 1894 (Tallahatchie, Mississippi, 1900 US census)
Bugger	**Bugger Cheeks** (male), born Georgia, c.1891 (Raiford, Georgia, 1910 US census)
Bum	**Bum Allgood**, born Georgia, c.1897 (Wild Cat, Georgia, 1910 US census)
Bumboy	**Oscar Bumboy Millard**, born Pennsylvania, c.1909 (Northumberland, Pennsylvania, 1910 US census)
Bummer	**Bummer Buffington**, born Louisiana, c.1843 (Bull Pond, South Carolina, 1880 US census). *Bummer was the father of Willie Buffington.*
Bumming	**Bumming Frederick**, born Great Hanningfield, Suffolk, c.1830 (Colchester, Essex, 1901 census)
Bush	**Bush Clit** (female), born c.1890 (Jackson, Georgia, 1920 US census)
	Bush Trimmer, born Alabama, c.1883 (Birmingham, Alabama, 1920 US census)
Carnal	**Carnal Jarvis**, born Wisbech, Cambridgeshire, 1852
Clit	**Clit Beatley**, born Carlton, Lincolnshire, c.1797 (Grainthorpe, Lincolnshire, 1871 census)
	Clit Bush, died Jackson, Georgia, USA, 14 November 1951

Cock	**Cock Smith**, born Yorkshire, *c.*1839 (Kirk Burton, Yorkshire, 1841 census)
Comes	**Comes More**, born Middlesex, *c.*1821 (Covent Garden, London, 1841 census)
Condoms	**Condoms Grace**, born Mississippi, *c.*1868 (Hamburg, Mississippi, 1880 US census)
Cunt, etc.	**Cunt Ah**, born China, *c.*1842 (Stanislaus, California, 1860 US census)
	Cunt Bates, born Louisiana, 1876 (De Soto, Louisiana, 1900 US census)
	Cunt Berger, born Germany, *c.*1878 (Sunderland, Durham, 1901 census)
	Cunt Pepper, born Smallthorne, Staffordshire, *c.*1828 (Burlsem, Staffordshire, 1851 census)
	Cunt Stubbee Billy, Private in Major Blue's detachment (Indiana, USA, War of 1812 service records)
	Cunts Goston de Arschot, born *c.*1849; passenger on *Normandie*, Le Havre, France–New York, USA, arrived 3 August 1885
	Cunts Munts, born Germany, *c.*1815 (Richfield, Washington, Wisconsin, 1850 US census)
	Cunty Hoel, born Warnham, Cheshire, *c.*1849 (Walton-on-the-Hill, Lancashire, 1871 census). *Cunty Hoel was the wife of Dick Hoel.*
	Cunty Young, born New Hampshire, *c.*1815 (Bradleysvale, Vermont, 1850 US census)
Fellate	**Fellate Dube**, born California, *c.*1874 (San Francisco, 1910 US census)

Forskin	**Forskin Maaskestad**, born Norway, c.1886; passenger on *Saxonia*, Liverpool, UK–New York, USA, arrived 5 February 1902
Fuck, etc.	**Fuck Ah**, born China, 6 June 1854 (New Westminster, British Columbia, 1901 Canada census)
	Fuck Hunt, born c.1834 (St Mary Newington, Surrey, 1841 census)
	Fuck Wang, born China, 1862 (Lewiston City, Nez Perce, Idaho, 1900 US census)
	Fuckem Mocher, born c.1873; passenger on *Lake Ontario*, Liverpool, UK–Montreal, Quebec, Canada, arrived 24 August 1900
	Fucker Tucker, born Hastings, Ontario, Canada, 7 August 1901
	Fuckie Offshlay, born Russia, c.1890 (New York, 1910 US census)
	Fuckyer Fritz, born c.1877; passenger on *New England*, Liverpool, UK–Boston, Massachusetts, USA, arrived 9 August 1901
	Fuk Mi, died British Columbia, Canada, 16 March 1894
	Fuk Yu, born China, c.1852 (Vancouver, British Columbia, 1901 Canada census)
	Fuku Nozwara Boogert, born 1935; died Hammersmith, London, 1988
Hampton	**Hampton Wick**, born South Carolina, c.1819 (Union, South Carolina, 1860 US census). *Hampton Wick is the London suburb that gave rise to the rhyming slang, Hampton Wick = prick. Mr Wick is a rare example of a person bearing this name.*
Hardon	**Hardon King**, born c.1828 (St James, Clerkenwell Green, London, 1841 census)

Horny	**Horny Cunt** (female), born *c.*1863 (Dakota Territory, 1886 US Indian census)
	Horny Ende, born Warwickshire, *c.*1830 (Birmingham, Warwickshire, 1841 census)
Humping	**Humping M. C. Palmer**, born Newbury, Berkshire, *c.*1872 (Newbury, 1881 census)
Knob	**Knob Hill Palmer**, born Uppingham, Rutland, 1905
Labia	**Labia Fannie**, (male), born Indiana, *c.*1883 (San Bernardino, California, 1900 US census)
	Labia Hood, born Nottingham, *c.*1843 (Snelland, Nottinghamshire, 1861 census)
Lesbiana	**Lesbiana Wharton**, born Ross, Herefordshire, *c.*1803 (Chelsea, London, 1881 census)
Merkin	**Merkin King**, born Nassington, Northamptonshire, *c.*1837 (Nassington, 1871 census)
Minge	**Minge Bacon**, born *c.*1910 (Nevada, 1912 US Indian census)
	Minge Semon, born *c.*1881 (Isleta, New Mexico, 1886 US Indian census)
	Minge Smith, born Crich, Derbyshire, *c.*1860 (Holbeck, Nottinghamshire, 1891 census)
Minkie	**Minkie Miles**, born Hammersmith, London, *c.*1895 (Fulham, London, 1901 census)
Nadger	**Nadger Patter**, born Ohio, *c.*1814 (Jefferson, Michigan, 1850 US census)
Oral	**Oral Love**, born Texas, *c.*1893 (Rockwall, Texas, 1910 US census)
	Oral Sexton, born 24 February 1904; died Collinsville, Illinois, USA, July 1976

Organ	**Organ B. Long**, married Jennie Pruett, Dekalb, Alabama, USA, 22 December 1893
	Organ Turner, born Mississippi, *c.*1896 (Pontotoc, Mississippi, 1910 US census)
Penis	**Penis Curling**, born Southall, Middlesex, *c.*1903 (Uxbridge, Middlesex, 1911 census)
	Penis Fannie, born North Carolina, *c.*1874 (Buncombe, North Carolina, 1910 US census)
	Penis Hardon, born Ireland, *c.*1811 (Fulham, London, 1851 census)
	Penis King, born North Carolina, *c.*1907 (Greenville, North Carolina, 1910 US census). *Penis was the daughter of Willy and Lovie King.*
	Penis Rough, born Ireland, *c.*1831 (Liverpool, Lancashire, 1871 census)
Poof	**Poof Helzer**, born Iowa, *c.*1859 (Marion, Iowa, 1860 US census)
Prick	**Prick Bishop**, born England, *c.*1831 (Carleton, 1891 Canada census)
	Prick Blair, born Kentucky, *c.*1852 (Colville, Washington, 1910 US census)
	Prick Green, born Preston, Lancashire, *c.*1863 (Clitheroe, Lancashire, 1881 census)
Pube	**Pube Brown**, born New York, *c.*1826 (Plymouth, New York, 1860 US census)
	Pube Russell, born Nova Scotia, Canada, 1904 (Lunenberg, Nova Scotia, 1911 Canada census)

Pussy	**Pussy Major**, born Georgia, *c.*1845 (Brownville and Whittens, Lee, Alabama, 1880 US census)
	Pussy Memory, born North Carolina, 1860 (Cumberland, North Carolina, 1860 US census)
	Pussy Small, born South Carolina, *c.*1830 (Beaufort, South Carolina, 1870 US census)
Semen	**Semen Brain**, born East Dean, Gloucestershire, *c.*1865 (East Dean, 1901 census)
	Semen Cox, born New Jersey, *c.*1875 (Lower, New Jersey, 1920 US census)
	Semen Fur, born 1913; died Bradford, Yorkshire, 2004
	Semen Kuntze, born Waterbury, Connecticut, USA, *c.*1906; passenger on *New York*, Southampton, England–New York, USA, arrived 28 February 1913
	Semen Sacks, born Illinois, *c.*1862 (Elbe, Washington, 1930 US census)
	Semen Smith, born Burrough on the Hill, Leicestershire, *c.*1834 (Burton upon Trent, Staffordshire, 1861 census)
	Semen Suk, born Grodno, Russia, *c.*1882; passenger on *Haverford*, Liverpool, England–Philadelphia, Pennsylvania, USA, arrived 17 June 1907
	Semen Tugwell, born Westonbirt, Gloucestershire, *c.*1794 (Frampton Cotterell, Gloucestershire, 1861 census)
Sex	**Sex Butter**, born Georgia, 1883 (Savannah, Georgia, 1900 US census)

Sexey	**Sexey Butt**, born Dundry, Somerset, *c*.1803 (Hanham, Gloucestershire, 1851 census)
Shag	**Shag Cummins**, born 12 April 1898; died Monahans, Texas, USA, March 1872
	Shag Suckerman, born North Dakota, *c*.1914 (Dickinson, North Dakota, 1920 US census)
Shagger	**Shagger Polos**, born Ontario, 1890 (Schreiber, Ontario, 1911 Canada census)
Spunk(y)	**Spunk Willis**, born Georgia, *c*.1873 (Daviston, Georgia, 1880 US census)
	Spunky Duncan, born Indiana, *c*.1860 (Harrison, Indiana, 1860 US census)
Stuffs	**Stuffs McAnally** (male), born Georgia, 1895 (Abbeville Town, Georgia, 1900 US census)
Suck, etc.	**Suck Kock**, born China, *c*.1892; passenger on *Nippon Maru*, Hong Kong–San Francisco, California, USA, arrived 22 September 1913
	Suckey Cox, born Georgia, *c*.1810 (Walton, Georgia, 1870 US census)
	Suckey Dick (female), born South Carolina, *c*.1840 (Swimming Pens, Sumter, South Carolina, 1870 US census)
	Sukey Cock, married Samuel Brown, St Mary, Truro, Cornwall, 27 March 1826
Tackle	**Tackle Nible**, born Sweden, *c*.1879 (Cherry Valley, Washington, 1910 US census)
Tit, etc.	**Tit Burkes**, born Alabama, 1895 (Perote, Alabama, 1900 US census)

Tit Jug, born Georgia, *c.*1890 (Blackwell, Georgia, 1910 US census)

Tit Minge, born Virginia, *c.*1871 (Tyler, Virginia, 1880 US census)

Tit Ouch, born Austria, *c.*1883 (Spokane, Washington, 1910 US census)

Tit Willis, born Sussex, 1897

Tits Cherrie, born Italy, *c.*1870 (Butler, Pennsylvania, 1910 US census)

Tits Tilles, born Rockingbourne, Hampshire, *c.*1878 (Fordingbridge, Hampshire, 1891 census)

Titties Wadsworth, born New York, *c.*1876 (Brooklyn, New York, 1910 US census)

Titz Craft, born Kentucky, 1899 (Raccoon, Kentucky, 1900 US census)

Tosser   **Tosser Smith**, born California, *c.*1838 (Sonoma, California, 1860 US census)

Sucker   **Sucker Willis**, born North Carolina, *c.*1896 (Smyrna, North Carolina, 1910 US census)

Vagina   **Vagina Glasscock**, born Alabama, *c.*1889 (Somerville, Morgan, Alabama, 1910 US census)

Vagina O'Hara, born *c.*1891 (San Francisco, California, 1920 US census)

Vagina Price, born Georgia, 1860 (Ring Jaw, Georgia, 1900 US census)

Vagina Smith, born Maryland, *c.*1824 (New York, 1870 US census)

Vulva   **Vulva Johnson**, died Baldwin, Alabama, USA, 6 July 1947

Wackoff	**Wackoff Roe**, resident of Monmouth, New Jersey, USA (1895 New Jersey state census)
Wank	**Wank Hardy**, born Idle, Yorkshire, *c.*1892 (Idle, 1901 census)
Wanker	**Wanker Collar**, born New York, *c.*1856 (Vevay, Michigan, 1910 US census)
Well Hung	**Well Hung**, born Texas, *c.*1867 (Harris, Texas, 1920 US census)

Initial Doubts

R.U. Ready for this? Parents seldom think beyond the baby's full name to consider its ramifications. Will the initials alone prompt some other association – think B.J., E.T., F.U., S.O.S., S.S. and so on – and what will be the effect of the first name appearing as an initial, or of a middle initial? Among those who ignored this basic tenet we may cite the following, albeit that some started out with the additional disadvantage of an unfortunate surname.

A. Biggerdyke
Born Moulton, Lincolnshire, *c.*1809
(Spalding, Lincolnshire, 1861 census)

A. Bitch
Married Racine, Wisconsin, USA, 8 April 1880

A. Blob
Born Yorkshire, *c.*1827
(Snaith, Yorkshire, 1841 census)

A. Certain Gaze
Born *c.*1788; died Norwich, Norfolk, 1871

A. Cunt
(Female) Baptized St James', Colchester,
Essex, 1 March 1684

A. Frump
Born North Petherton, Somerset, *c.*1841
(North Petherton, 1851 census)

A. Goodlay
Born Ireland, *c.*1832
(St Louis, Missouri, 1860 US census)

A. Harry Botty
Born Bethnal Green, London, 1884

A. Hitman
>Baptized St George in the East,
>London, 12 November 1775

A. Hugass
>Born Sweden, c.1905; crew on *City of New York*,
>Sweden–New York, USA, arrived 25 April 1932

A. Level
>Baptized Sudbury, Suffolk, 19 January 1792

A. Little Lowder
>Born Kansas, USA, 31 July 1877
>(World War I draft registration)

A. Lotta Slut
>Born Vaasa, Finland, 9 February 1827

A. Lovely Day
>Born Alaska, 17 October 1895; died Los Angeles,
>California, USA, 14 March 1986

A. Men
>Born Cornwall, c.1840
>(Camborne, Cornwall, 1841 census)

Ana L. Brown
>Born Lynesack and Softly, Durham, c.1900
>(Lynesack and Softly, 1901 census)

A. Pervert
>Married George Kelway, Yeovil, Somerset,
>15 April 1816

A. Quaintance
>Born 29 October 1917; died Boulder, Montana,
>USA, 20 February 1998

Ars E. Eaton
>Born c.1914
>(Burlinton, Des Moines, Iowa, 1930 US census)

A. Twat
>Born Orkney and Shetland, Scotland, c.1814
>(Foula, Sandness, Papa Stour and Walls, Orkney
>and Shetland, 1841 Scotland census)

B. Ann Angel
> Born Bedwelty, Monmouthshire, 1894

B. Astard
> Born Staffordshire, c.1826
> (West Bromwich, Staffordshire, 1841 census)

B. Have
> Born 26 August 1787; baptized St Mary's
> Independent, Glossop, Derbyshire, September 1787

B. Hive
> Married Thomas Redding, Stepney,
> London, 17 August 1656

B. Quick
> Born Ireland, c.1822
> (Tower Hamlets, London, 1881 census)

B. Ware
> Baptized St John the Baptist, Leytonstone,
> Essex, 14 June 1891

B. Yond
> Born Prescot, Lancashire, 1905

C. Below
> Married John Howell, St Bride Fleet Street,
> London, 8 November 1808

C. Cret
> Born c.1872 (Pratt, West Virginia, 1930 US census)

C. Litoris
> Baptized Liebfrauen Katholisch, Koblenz,
> Prussia, 29 September 1602

C. Rap
> Born Bethnal Green, London, c.1831
> (Bethnal Green, 1881 census)

C. Saw
> Born Edmonton, Middlesex, 1879

C. Senor
> Born Middlesex, c.1831
> (Clerkenwell, London, 1841 census)

C. Side
Born St Saviour, Southwark, London, 1841

D. C. Washington
Born 13 July 1903; died Monroe,
Louisiana, USA, 27 April 1991

D. Viant
(Male) Born Stoke Damerel, Devon, 1857

E. C. Lay
(Female) Born Lizard, Cornwall, *c.*1862
(Pendeen, Cornwall, 1871 census)

E. Coli
Baptized Waltham Abbey, Essex, 27 October 1746

E. I. M. Cumming
Born Scotland, *c.*1865
(Camberwell, London, 1891 census)

E. Lastic
Born 16 September 1923; died Ohio, USA, July 1972

E. Love Cock
Born St Pancras, London, *c.*1869
(Shoreditch, London, 1901 census)

E. Mail
Born Malmesbury, Wiltshire,
1855

E. Normus Carpenter
Born 25 May 1866; died Boise,
Idaho, USA, 3 November 1936

E. Rect
Born Iowa, *c.*1910
(Shenandoah, Iowa, 1930 US census)

E. Vil
Born Hermitage, Staffordshire, *c.*1864
(Nottingham, 1881 census)

F. Ewe
Married St Pancras, London, 1899

F. Ing
>Baptized Blean, Kent, 21 June 1829

F. Ingood
>Born Tutbury, Staffordshire, c.1851
>(Burton upon Trent, Staffordshire, 1861 census)

F. Off
>Baptized Ampthill, Bedfordshire, 14 February 1875

F. Uckwell
>Born Barton, Oxfordshire, c.1859
>(Steeple Barton, Oxfordshire, 1861 census)

G. Force
>Born 12 December 1945; died Ohio,
>USA, 15 May 1990

G. Raffe
>Born 10 June 1896; died Chicago,
>Illinois, USA, February 1975

G. Roper
>(Male) Baptized St Margaret, Westminster,
>London, 22 May 1552

G. Spot
>Baptized Edinburgh, Midlothian, 1 July 1621

G. Wizz
>Born Austria, c.1891
>(Cambria, Pennsylvania, 1910 US census)

I. Brow
>Baptized Old Machar, Aberdeen, 20 August 1724

I. Doshit
>Born Louisiana, c.1889
>(New Orleans, Louisiana, 1910 US census)

I. Dunnit
>Born Paisley, Renfrewshire, 9 October 1812

I. Lash
>Born Poplar, London, c.1890
>(Wanstead, Essex, 1901 census)

I. Level
   Born Hutchesontown, Glasgow, 10 December 1859

I. Lid
   Born Tomrefjord, Norway, 18 July 1847

I. Lovit
   Married Mary Mothersell, Harlington, Bedfordshire, 13 June 1710

I. M. Ready
   Born 21 March 1913; died Iron Mountain, Michigan, USA, 16 February 1991

I. Owa
   Born Hawaii, c.1901 (Kaapoko, Hawaii, 1910 US census)

I. P. Freely
   Born New York, c.1898 (New York, 1930 US census)

I. Pad
   Born 11 November 1944; died Toa Alta, Puerto Rico, 30 August 2009

I. Phone
   Born Romania, c.1881 (Bronx, New York, 1920 US census)

I. Pod
   Baptized Whatfield, Suffolk, 20 May 1638

GOODNIGHT

CAPYRIGHT 1880.

I. Scream
Baptized Paisley Abbey,
Renfrewshire,
23 May 1824

I. Sickle
Born Newcastle upon
Tyne, Northumberland,
c.1857 (Washington,
Durham, 1871 census)

I. Sight
Born Shirley, Hampshire,
c.1895 (Shirley, 1901
census)

I. Tunes
Married Durham, 1874

L. E. Gover
(Female) Born South
Stoneham,
Hampshire, 1894

Lesbia N. Wall
Born 20 February 1843;
died Columbia, Maury,
Tennessee, USA,
25 May 2006

L. Plate
Born Sussex, c.1811
(Warminghurst,
Sussex, 1841 census)

M. Aine
Born Spain, c.1828
(New York, 1860 US
census)

M. Inge
(Female), born Eastry,
Kent, 1840

Ming E. King
  Born Pennsylvania, *c.*1875
  (Latrobe, Pennsylvania, 1910 US census)

N. Gorge
  Born Norfolk, *c.*1840 (Larling, Norfolk, 1841 census)

N. Obrain
  Born Ontario, *c.*1857
  (Goderich Town, Ontario, Canada 1871 census)

O. Dear
  Born Stotfold, Bedfordshire, *c.*1886
  (Stotfold, 1891 census)

O. Heck
  Born Leeds, *c.*1836
  (Headingley cum Burley, Yorkshire, 1901 census)

O. Hell
  Baptized Old Meeting Gaol Street Presbyterian,
  Great Yarmouth, Norfolk, 24 February 1709

O. Hio
  Born New York, *c.*1847
  (Fulton, New York, 1910 US census)

O. Men
  Born Blackfriars, London, *c.*1870
  (Southwark, London, 1881 census)

P. Enis
  (Male) Born Lancashire, *c.*1806
  (Manchester, Lancashire, 1841 census)

Peni S. Johnsen
  Passenger on *Amerika*, Arfendal, Norway–New
  Orleans, Louisiana, USA, arrived 7 November 1850

P. Freely
  Born Liverpool, Lancashire, 1841

P. Hole
  (Female) Married Wincanton, Somerset, 1842

P. Nile
  (Male) Born St Austell, Cornwall, 1897

P. Niss
Born Copenhagen, Denmark, 31 October 1889

P. Nutt
Born Macclesfield, Cheshire, 1859

P. Orridge
Born Chesterfield, Derbyshire, 1894

P. Rick
Married Ann Gouding, St Dunstan, Stepney,
London, 29 March 1835

P. Upward
Baptized Stourpaine, Dorset, 25 December 1867

R. M. Pitt
Born Wolverhampton, Staffordshire, 1904

R. Sitch
Born Lambeth, London, 1883

R. Slicker
Died Bradford, Yorkshire, 1876

R. Sole
Baptized St Martin-in-the-Fields, London,
5 August 1582

R. Soles
Born Greenwich, London, 1844

R. U. Ready
Born Kansas, c.1896 (Jefferson, Kansas,
1910 US census)

S. Emen
Born Brill, Buckinghamshire, c.1790
(Tring, Hertfordshire, 1851 census)

S. Hag
Married Henry Beerlin, St Mary the Virgin,
Dover, Kent, 2 January 1800

S. Hagger
Baptized Great Chishall, Essex, 7 May 1646

S. Hit
>Born London, c.1862
>(Kensington, London, 1871 census)

Shi T. Huang
>Born 15 January 1932; died Bronx, New York,
>USA, 6 May 2005

S. Melly
>Born Liverpool, Lancashire, 1871

S. Trumpet
>(Female) Born Tynemouth, Northumberland, 1862

T. Caddy
>Born Beaminster, Somerset, 1841

T. Cosy
>Born South Molton, Devon, c.1820
>(South Molton, 1881 census)

T. Cupp
>Born Beaminster, Dorset, 1876

T. Hee
>Born Nafferton, Yorkshire, c.1891
>(Great Driffield, Yorkshire, 1901 census)

T. Nager
>Baptized Lugershall, Buckinghamshire, 17 July 1603

T. Shirt
>Born Ecclesfield, Yorkshire, 1843

T. Time
>Married Anne Delloe, Furneaux Pelham,
>Hertfordshire, 26 April 1618

T. Towel
>Married Deborah Handsley, Freiston,
>Lincolnshire, 13 May 1783

T. Vee
>Born Boston, Lincolnshire, c.1804
>(Skirbeck, Lincolnshire, 1851 census)

U. Bend
> Born Canada, 1849
> (Gaspé, Canada, 1861 Canada census)

U. Watt
> Married Castle Ward, Northumberland, 1900

V. Longcock
> (Male) Born c.1876; passenger on *Lake Winnipeg*,
> Quebec, Canada-Liverpool, England, arrived October
> 1897

V. Sign
> Born Lewisham, London, 1895

W. Ank
> Born 4 September 1947; died Pennsylvania,
> USA, 19 August 2009

W. Anker
> (Male) Baptized Wonersh, Surrey, 28 July 1877

Wan K. Richards
> Born Maine, c.1889
> (Sheburne, Massachusetts, 1920 US census)

W. C. Weewie Born c.1904; died Everett, Washington,
USA, 2 February 1981

W. W. Web Born Georgia, c.1845
> (Baker, Georgia, 1850 US census)

X. Ray
> Born New York, c.1876 (New York, 1880 US census)

Y. Mee
> Born 1936; died Stoke-on-Trent, Staffordshire, 1997

Y. Nott
> Born 1930; died Tunbridge Wells, Kent, 2002

It's Not Fair: Unfortunate Name Combinations

You may be lucky enough to have an innocuous surname, in which case your choice of first names for your baby is infinite. But, as with the initials, while all those that follow are fairly common first names, it is the combination with the surname that causes problems and produces unintended results – with which the child is stuck, perhaps for life. It may be tempting, but if you happen to have a surname that when combined with a first name sounds like some common word or phrase, avoid it at all costs. Imagine if your surname was 'Inch' and you called your daughter 'Ann', so that every time anyone hears the name they remark, 'Give her an inch and she'll take a mile!' The poor girl will go through life with a rictus smile as people expect her to laugh as though she has just heard it for the first time. Similarly, 'Seymour Butts', though redolent of a Bart Simpson prank phone call, is a real name, along with many others, where deliberately (or, more commonly, accidentally) the unfortunate child ended up with a name akin to these relatively recent and genuine exemplars: Connie Lingus, Ina Buckett, Tanya Hyde, Stu Pidd, Dinah Might, Jack B. Nimble, Rusty Nail, Jack D. Ripper, Ann Droid, Dawn Raid, Phil Mike Hunt, Cindy Doll, Chris P. Duck, Lynne C. Doyle, Gay Man, Stan Dupp, Justin Time and Crystal Clear.

A game for all the family (except the children) – cover either the first names or surnames and guess what they ended up with.

Ada

Sounding so like 'had a...', this three-letter palindromic name has potential for all manner of double entendre interpretations

Ada Cock, born Penzance, Cornwall, 1866

Ada Pee, born Manchester, *c.*1892 (Manchester, 1911 census)

Ada Poo, born Poplar, London, *c.*1889 (Poplar, 1911 census)

Ada Prick, born *c.*1878; died Sheffield, 1907

Ada Tantrum, born Ludlow, Shropshire, 1875

Agusta	**Agusta Wind**, born Prussia, c.1850 (Hurricane, Illinois, 1880 US census). *Note the name of the town in which she lived.*
Al	**Al Aska**, born 5 November 1901; died New York, USA, August 1955
	Al Bino, born St Marylebone, London, c.1860 (Southwark, London, 1871 census)
	Al Dente, born Whitechapel, London, c.1900 (St Botolph, Aldersgate, London, 1901 census)
	Al Fresco, born St Giles, London, 1853
Alan	**Alan Key**, born Poole, Dorset, 1900
Albert	**Albert Hall**, baptized St Martin in the Fields, London, 26 October 1600
Alf	**Alf Abbet**, born Teddington, Middlesex, c.1849 (Teddington, 1891 census)
Ali/Allie/ Ally	**Ali Barber**, baptized Inveresk with Musselburgh, Midlothian, 29 August 1731
	Ali Katt (female), born Axminster, Devon, c.1819 (Lyme, Dorset, 1871 census)
	Allie Bama, born Texas, c.1898 (Blossom, Texas, 1910 US census)
	Ally Way, born 18 April 1948; died Winchester, Hampshire, December 1998
Alice	**Alice Wonderland**, born New Jersey, 1890 (Chester, New Jersey, 1900 US census)
Alice May	**Alice May Fall**, born Shoreditch, London, 1894
	Alice May Pee, born Cheslyn Hay, Staffordshire, c.1902 (Cheslyn Hay, 1911 census)
	Alice May Poke, born Sheffield, Yorkshire, 1896
Amanda	**Amanda Lynn**, born 27 September 1884; died Pittsburgh, Pennsylvania, USA, February 1973

Andy	**Andy Tover**, born Warwickshire, c.1821 (Birmingham, Warwickshire, 1841 census)
Anice	**Anice Bottom**, baptized Thornhill by Dewsbury, Yorkshire, 14 May 1837
	Anice Pair, born Georgia, c.1889 (Scottsboro, Alabama, 1920 US census)
Anita *Sounds too much like 'I need a...'*	**Anita Bath**, born Wisconsin, c.1902 (Milwaukee, Wisconsin, 1920 US census)
	Anita Beaver, born Wisconsin, c.1904 (Granton, Wisconsin, 1920 US census)
	Anita Date, born Edmonton, Middlesex, 1893
	Anita Dick, born Mississippi, c.1889 (Jackson, Mississippi, 1910 US census)
	Anita Hooker, born Louisiana, c.1907 (New Orleans, Louisiana, 1910 US census)
	Anita Porno, born Santa Fe, c.1891 (Santa Fe, 1895 Argentina census)
Ann/Anna	**Ann Ally**, born Massachusetts, c.1820 (Lynn, Massachusetts, 1870 US census)
	Ann Ambush, born Maryland, c.1825 (Newburyport, Massachusetts, 1870 US census)
	Ann Ant, born Wadena, Minnesota, USA, 3 September 1893; died Minneapolis, Minnesota, July 1982
	Ann Archy, born Haslingden, Lancashire, 1886
	Ann Chovey, born France, c.1810 (Fort Wayne, Indiana, 1880 US census)
	Ann Eel, baptized Watlington, Oxfordshire, 16 February 1812
	Ann Eraser, married John Mackie, Aberdeen, 13 May 1831

Ann Inch, baptized St Kew, Cornwall,
16 February 1713

Ann Nus, married John Dixon, St Peter-at-
Leeds, Leeds, Yorkshire, 4 February 1671

Ann Ode, born West Derby, Lancashire, 1846

Ann Other, died Leyburn, Yorkshire, 1899

Ann Teater, born Lamberhurst, Sussex,
c.1854 (Tonbridge, Kent, 1881 census)

Anna Conder, born Mile End, London, c.1794
(West Ham, Essex, 1851 census)

Anna Gram, born c.1811 (Ambrosden,
Oxfordshire, 1841 census)

Anna Rack, married St George in the East,
London, 1881

Anna Sasin, born Austria, c.1882
(Clayton, Michigan, 1910 US census)

Annie   **Annie Body**, born Plympton St Mary,
Devon, 1866

Annie Bodys, born Neilston, Renfrewshire,
c.1844 (Barrhead and Levern, 1901 Scotland
census). *She had a daughter who was also
Annie Bodys.*

Annie Fucks, born c.1872; passenger on *Lake
Ontario*, Liverpool, England–Halifax, Nova
Scotia, Canada, arrived 7 December 1900

Annie How, born Ecclesfield, Yorkshire, 1843

Annie Moment, born Georgia, c.1882
(Wrightsboro, Georgia, 1910 US census)

Annette   **Annette Curtain**, born South Carolina,
c.1896, (New York, 1920 US census)

April   **April Showers**, born 27 February 1956; died
Wilmington, California, USA, 16 May 2008

Arthur	**Arthur Mind**, born Poplar, London, 1907
	Arthur Minute, born Hastings, Sussex, 1882
	Arthur Pint, born Portsmouth, Hampshire, c.1797 ('brewer', Portsea, Hampshire, 1851 census)
Asa	**Asa Hole**, born Idaho, c.1898 (Spokane, Washington, 1910 US census)
Ava	**Ava Bang**, born Yugoslavia, c.1903; passenger on *Melita*, Antwerp, Belgium–Montreal, Canada, arrived 15 May 1926
Barb	**Barb B. Doll**, born 25 September 1907; died Billings, Montana, USA, June 1989
	Barb Dwyer, baptized Sacred Heart and English Martyrs, Thornley, Durham, 7 January 1877
	Barb Wire, died Birmingham, Warwickshire, 1916
Barbara	**Barbara Seville**, born Birkenhead, Cheshire, c.1882 (Birkenhead, 1901 census)
Barbie	**Barbie Cue**, born Scotland, c.1819 (Philadelphia, Pennsylvania, 1880 US census)
	Barbie Doll, born 28 July 1898; died Kingston, New York, USA, October 1975
Barry	**Barry Cade**, born 13 February 1948; died Princeton, Illinois, USA, 15 May 2008
Basil	**Basil Leaf**, born York, 1895
Baxter	**Baxter Wall**, born West Ham, Essex, 1906
Bea	**Bea Hives**, born Lambeth, London, 1887
	Bea Low, baptized Winwick, Lancashire, 18 October 1706
	Bea Sting, born c.1905 (Manchester, New Hampshire, 1930 US census)

Bellah	**Bellah Bottoms**, born Skipton, Yorkshire, *c.*1803 (Bingley, Yorkshire, 1851 census)
Belle	**Belle Button**, born Salehurst, Sussex, *c.*1873 (Salehurst, 1891 census)
Ben/Benny	**Ben Dover**, baptized St George in the East, London, 10 March 1839
	Ben Nevis, born France, *c.*1845 (St Mary in the Castle, Hastings, Sussex, 1871 census)
	Benny Fitt, born Shoreditch, London, 1876
Bertha	**Bertha Bangs**, born Nebraska, *c.*1885 (Lincoln, Nebraska, 1910 US census)
Bess	**Bess Befor**, baptized St Giles without Cripplegate, London, 26 July 1629
Betty	**Betty Swall**, married Auckland, Durham, 1860. *This name is notable as a potential spoonerism.*
Bill	**Bill Board**, born Abergavenny, Monmouthshire, *c.*1890 (Abergavenny, 1891 Wales census)
	Bill Ding, baptized Easton-on-the-Hill, Northamptonshire, 22 September 1661
Bing	**Bing Bong**, born China, 14 August 1874 (Vancouver, British Columbia, 1901 Canada census)
	Bing Go, born 10 May 1903; died Minneapolis, Minnesota, USA, 6 June 1990
Bob/Bobby	**Bob A. Job**, born Sunderland, Durham, *c.*1878 (Sunderland, 1901 census)
	Bob Builder, married Susanna Sproll, St Philip and St Jacob, Bristol, Gloucestershire, 8 October 1778
	Bob Sleigh, baptized Edinburgh, Midlothian, 6 November 1608

Buster	**Buster Cherry**, born Mississippi, c.1880 (Lee, Mississippi, 1920 US census)
Cairy/ Carie/ Carrie	**Cairy Hunt**, born Kentucky, 1884 (Nicholas, Kentucky, 1900 US census). *A spooneristic name.*
	Carie Mycock, born Saskatchewan, c.1909 (Regina, Saskatchewan, Canada, 1916 Manitoba, Saskatchewan and Alberta census)
	Carrie Oke, born Bideford, Devon, 1864
Cali	**Cali Fornia**, born Arizona, c.1886 (Seattle, Washington, 1910 US census)
Carol	**Carol Service**, born 20 October 1932; died Willington, Connecticut, USA, 14 April 1997
	Carol Singer, died Newport, Monmouthshire, 1998
Cat	**Cat Basket**, married Robert Girling, St Matthew, Ipswich, Suffolk, 19 November 1764
Cath	**Cath Ode**, born Wigan, Lancashire, 1898
Catherine	**Catherine Wheel**, born Auckland, Durham, 1867

Charity	**Charity Chilly**, baptized Menheniot, Cornwall, 24 November 1736. *Her parents, Nicholas and Charity, were perhaps inspired by the expression 'as cold as charity'.*
Charlotte	**Charlotte Gobbles**, born Chatham, Kent, c.1873 (Chatham, 1891 census)
	Charlotte May Stuff, born Greenwich, London, 1894
Cherie	**Cherie Pye**, born 25 February 1933; died Carmel, Indiana, USA, 6 October 2009
Chip	**Chip Wood**, born Huddersfield, Yorkshire, 1867
Chris	**Chris Cross**, born Ireland, c.1872 (New York, 1910 US census)
	Chris Mass, born Asenby, Yorkshire, c.1839 (Lamesley, Durham, 1861 census)
	Chris P. Bacon, born 7 April 1920; died South Burlington, Vermont, USA, 30 January 1997
	Chris Peacock, born Askrigg, Yorkshire, 1837
Christian	**Christian Charity**, baptized Hollesley, Suffolk, 19 December 1731
Christiana	**Christiana Whores**, married Johes [sic] Touse, St George, Wilton, Somerset, 25 April 1585
Chuck	**Chuck Stone**, born 30 September 1926; died Julesberg, Colorado, USA, 30 July 1998
Claude	**Claude Balls**, born Texas, c.1908 (Houston, Texas, 1930 US census)
	Claude Crabb, born London, c.1875 (Stratford, London, 1901 census)
	Claude Pecker, born Atcham, Shropshire, 1897

Cliff	**Cliff Edge**, born Haslingden, Lancashire, 1903
	Cliff Hanger, born Ohio, c.1893 (McDonald, Ohio, 1910 US census)
Connie	**Connie Linger**, born Wolverhampton, Staffordshire, c.1889 (Birmingham, Warwickshire, 1891 census)
Crystal	**Crystal Ball**, born Nebraska, c.1908 (Gage, Nebraska, 1920 US census). *Her sister was called Merlin Ball.*
Daisy	**Daisy Chain**, born Kansas, c.1886 (Dallas, Texas, 1920 US census)
Dan	**Dan D. Lyons**, born Cardiff, Glamorgan, 1891 (Cardiff, 1891 Wales census)
	Dan Druff, born Kentucky, c.1841 (Perry, Kentucky, 1850 US census)
	Dan Ger, born Devon, c.1796 (Roborough, Devon, 1841 census)
Debbie	**Debbie Gulps**, born New York, USA, c.1861; married Benjamine [*sic*] Palmer, Sparta, Michigan, 18 February 1877
Dee	**Dee Light**, born 1964; died Hackney, London, 2004
Della	**Della Ware**, born 27 October 1889; died Saegertown, Pennsylvania, USA, February 1969
Des	**Des Troyer**, born 9 April 1888; died Goshen, Indiana, USA, February 1979
Desire	**Desire Bush**, born New York, c.1855 (Olive, New York, 1870 US census)
Désiré	**Désiré de Cock**, married Armandine Viard, Paris, France, 20 April 1891

Dick:
Richard is a fine name, and its inevitable abbreviation to Dick is fine too – but not if your surname happens to conjure up an unintended image

Dick Anybody, married Margreett [*sic*] Gaskine, Rowley Regis, Staffordshire, 1 January 1668

Dick Ass, born Kolberg, Prussia, 23 November 1881; died 24 November 1941

Dick Balling, born Alabama, 1909 (Greenville, Alabama, 1910 US census)

Dick Bangs, born West Ham, London, 1910

Dick Beater, born Norwich, Norfolk, c.1835 (Wisbech, Norfolk, 1851 census). *At the time of the census, Dick Beater was a sixteen-year-old prisoner in Wisbech jail.*

Dick Bellend, baptized St Mary Magdalene, Bermondsey, London, 6 February 1848

Dick Bigrigg, born Gateshead, Durham, 1893

Dick Blower, baptized Roxwell, Essex, 19 September 1559

Dick Bollock, married Dorathy [*sic*] Marten, St Mabyn, Cornwall, 16 June 1659

Dick Boner, born Indiana, c.1910 (Allen, Indiana, 1920 US census)

Dick Brain, born Stoke-on-Trent, Staffordshire, 1871

Dick Bumming, born Clam Union, Missaukee, Michigan, USA, 9 March 1894

Dick Cheese, born Georgia, 1867 (Nance, Georgia, 1900 US census)

Dick Clap, married Mary Blake, Boston, Massachusetts, USA, 26 September 1807

Dick Cockout, baptized Manchester Cathedral, Manchester, Lancashire, 17 May 1796

Dick Comes, born Thorpe, Surrey, c.1798 (Thorpe, 1851 census). *Dick Comes was the father of Willy Comes.*

Dick Condom, born St Marylebone, Middlesex, c.1845 (St Marylebone, 1851 census)

Dick Dangle, born 24 July 1930; died Carrolton, Georgia, USA, 30 April 2003

Dick Dick, born Coylton, Ayr, 19 February 1856

Dick Eater, born Ruislip, Middlesex, c.1829 (Ruislip, 1851 census)

Dick End, married Sarah Hunt, Lacock, Wiltshire, 21 July 1755

Dick Everhard, married Frances Lee, Billesley, Warwickshire, 11 September 1653

Dick Face, baptized Ridgmont, Bedfordshire, 14 July 1551

Dick Firm, born c.1861 (Penge, London, 1891 census)

Dick Fits, born Sandown Township, Rockingham, New Hampshire, America, 8 August 1758

Dick Gobling, born Croydon, Surrey, c.1810 (Lewisham, London, 1881 census)

Dick Gothard, born Ely, Cambridgeshire, 1838

Dick Handler, baptized Earls Colne, Essex, 29 December 1585

Dick Hardcock, born c.1791 (Cheltenham, Gloucestershire, 1841 census)

Dick Hardon, buried Auckland, Durham, 25 April 1571

Dick Head, born Wandsworth, London, 1890

Dick Helmet, born Russia, c.1898; passenger on *Prinz Friedrich Wilhelm*, Bremen, Germany-New York, USA, arrived 8 May 1911

Dick Inass, born Washington, c.1877 (Lewis, Washington, 1880 US census)

Dick Ing, baptized Long Crendon, Buckinghamshire, 1 February 1858

Dick Inman, born Manchester, c.1872 (Chorlton, Lancashire, 1891 census)

Dick Justin, baptized St Andrew, Holborn, London, 4 October 1685

Dick Knob, married Elizabeth Flower, Beeston, Nottinghamshire, 14 November 1682

Dick Kunt, born Banwell, Somerset, c.1780 (Banwell, 1851 census)

Dick Licker, born Oldham, Lancashire, c.1845 (Oldham, 1861 census)

Dick Licks, married Jenny Clen-Quit-Sun, Clallam, Washington, USA, 18 May 1878

Dick Lover, baptized Thakeham, Sussex, 22 April 1591

Dick Massage, born 25 September 1737; baptized St Martin Vintry, London, 9 October 1737

Dick Muncher, born Welshampton, Shropshire, c.1838 (Horseman's Green, Flintshire, 1891 Wales census)

Dick Myass, baptized Hornsea, Yorkshire, 26 January 1804

Dick Nothard, born Sculcoates, Yorkshire, 1853

Dick Pounder, born Sculcoates, Yorkshire, 1903

Dick Prick, born c.1790; died Machynlleth, Powys, 1870

Dick Pumper, born Clee Hills, Shropshire, c.1826 (Kingswinford, Staffordshire, 1851 census)

Dick Rampant, father of Mary Rampant, baptized Dorking, Surrey, 21 February 1713

Dick Ramrod, born Swansea, Glamorgan, c.1847 (Merthyr Tydfil, Glamorgan, 1861 Wales census)

Dick Rash, born Chesterton, Cambridgeshire, 1872

Dick Rider, born Hungerford, Berkshire, 1839

Dick Shaft, born Littleover, Derbyshire, c.1883 (Derby, 1901 census)

Dick Shaker, baptized Fenny Compton, Warwickshire, 5 November 1772

Dick Shaver, born Alabama, c.1817 (Montgomery, Alabama, 1870 US census)

Dick Sprinkles, born Castle Thorpe, Buckinghamshire, c.1804 (Castle Thorpe, 1871 census)

Dick Stiff, born St Luke, Middlesex, 1846

Dick Stillhard, born 3 July 1913; died Rochester, New York, USA, 11 November 1993

Dick Stroker, baptized St Nicholas, Durham, 4 March 1642

Dick Sucker, baptized Weobley, Herefordshire, 21 January 1719

Dick Suckwell, born c.1785 (Potterspury, Northamptonshire, 1841 census)

Dick Surprise, born Cheshire, c.1822 (Chester, Cheshire, 1851 census)

Dick Swinger, born Norfolk, c.1821 (King's Lynn, Norfolk, 1841 census)

Dick Tater, married Elizabeth Wayman, Elmore, Gloucester, 23 April 1621

Dick Thrust, Goudhurst, Kent, 1598 (will)

Dick Tickler, baptized Sutton le Marsh, Lincolnshire, 11 May 1707

Dick Tosser, married Rebaka [sic] Tothill, Ideford, Devon, 13 April 1685

Dick Trickle, born Lancashire, c.1781 (Prescot, Lancashire, 1841 census). *His son was also called Dick Trickle.*

Dick Upright, born Exeter, Devon, 1862

Dick Wacker, born Essex, c.1781 (Dagenham, Essex, 1841 census)

Dick Wart, born Northamptonshire, c.1811 (Silverstone, Northamptonshire, 1841 census)

Dick Willy Cock, born Plymouth, Devon, 1853. *His name is a rare example of a penile triple.*

Dicky	**Dicky Bird**, born Edmonton, Middlesex, 1894
	Dicky Hart, born Mile End, London, c.1888 (Bethnal Green, London, 1891 census)
Dina(h)	**Dina Plate**, born Wisconsin, c.1872 (Rantoul, Wisconsin, 1880 US census)
	Dina Soares, born 1 August 1894; died Somerset, Massachusetts, USA, 14 May 1973
	Dinah Saw, baptized St Lawrence, Chobham, Surrey, 18 October 1818
Don	**Don Key**, born Norwich, Norfolk, 1885
Dora	**Dora Knob**, born Ohio, 1891 (McLean, Ohio, 1900 US census)
	Dora Mat, born Austria, c.1892 (Manhattan, New York, 1910 US census)
Dot	**Dot Com**, born Nebraska, c.1887 (Milton, Wisconsin, 1905 Wisconsin, USA, census)
Doug	**Doug Hole**, born Manchester, Lancashire, c.1910 (Manchester 1911 census)
Drew	**Drew Peacock**, born North Carolina, 1870 (Wilson, North Carolina, 1900 US census)
	Drew Pee, born c.1898 (Dent, Arkansas, 1930 US census)

Earl	**Earl E. Sex**, born 22 September 1919; died Licking, Ohio, USA, 19 March 2003
Earnest/ Ernest	**Earnest Lecher**, born c.1910 (Easton, Pennsylvania, 1930 US census)
	Earnest Willie Fuck, born Davenport, Iowa, USA, 23 February 1895
	Ernest Fucks, born Germany, c.1882 (Maidstone, Kent, 1911 census)
	Ernest Laughter, born Bromsgrove, Worcestershire, c.1880 (Bromsgrove, 1881 census)
	Ernest Shag, born Germany, c.1905 (Cheyenne, Laramie, Wyoming, 1920 US census)
Ed	**Ed Banger**, baptized North Petherton, Somerset, 4 February 1635
Eileen	**Eileen Back**, born Merthyr Tydfil, Glamorgan, 1908
	Eileen Dover, born 1924; died Swindon, Wiltshire, 1987
Eliza	**Eliza Scrack**, born Cuckfield, Sussex, 1873
Elizabeth	**Elizabeth Fuxall**, born Ohio, c.1830 (South Wheeling, Ohio, 1860 US census)
	Elizabeth Lovescock, baptized St Giles Cripplegate, London, 21 February 1727
	Elizabeth Scock, married Phillip Postle, Great Yarmouth, Norfolk, 29 September 1745
	Elizabeth Snickers, married Robert Musgrave, Burneston, Yorkshire, 20 December 1751
Elle/Ellie	**Elle Fant**, born Durham, 1861
	Elle Vator, born Newhaven, Sussex, c.1858 (Brighton, Sussex, 1881 census)
	Ellie Gant (male), born Tennessee, c.1864 (Fayette, Tennessee, 1870 US census)

Emma	**Emma Chiset**, born Brighton, Sussex, *c.*1828 (Brighton, 1851 census)
	Emma Royds, born Rochdale, Lancashire, 1838
	Emma Scunt, born Harrow, Middlesex, *c.*1845 (Stepney, London, 1861 census)
Eric	**Eric Schon**, born Germany, *c.*1878; passenger on *Frederich der Grosse*, Bremen, Germany–New York, USA, arrived 8 July 1897
Estelle	**Estelle Hurts**, born Sandal Magna, Yorkshire, *c.*1886 (Sandal Magna, 1891 census)
Esther	**Esther Bonnet**, born Rochdale, Lancashire, *c.*1886 (Rochdale, 1891 census)
	Esther Egg, married Glanford Brigg, Lincolnshire, 1863
	Esther Rabbit, born Gouldstone, Kent, *c.*1836 (Orpington, Kent, 1861 census)

Eta/Etta	**Eta Willey**, born Upottery, Devon, *c*.1888 (Upottery, 1891 census)
	Etta Banana, born 17 June 1920; died Miami, Florida, USA, 9 May 1994
	Etta Beaver, born Bradford, Yorkshire, 1895
	Etta Bottom, born Huddersfield, Yorkshire, *c*.1871 (Almondbury, Yorkshire, 1901 census)
	Etta Cherry, born 28 April 1898; died Jamaica, New York, USA, August 1977
	Etta Chicken, born Russia, *c*.1883 (Chicago, Illinois, 1910 US census)
	Etta De Cow, born Des Moines, Iowa, USA, *c*.1883 (Des Moines, 1925 Iowa state census)
	Etta Duck, born 4 December 1921; died Suffolk, Virginia, USA, 12 December 1999
	Etta Lott, born Mississippi, *c*.1877 (Lamar Mississippi, 1920 US census)
	Etta Nipples, born *c*.1897 (Escambia, Florida, USA, 1935 Florida state census)
Ethel	**Ethel Red**, born Kentish Town, London, *c*.1900 (St Pancras, London, 1901 census)
Eunice	**Eunice Bottom**, married Henry Badger, Peru, Massachusetts, USA, 18 September 1787
Eva	**Eva Brick**, born Turkey, *c*.1874 (Battersea, London, 1901 census)
	Eva Faithfull, born Winchester, Hampshire, 1895
	Eva Ready, born Halifax, Yorkshire, 1896
Everard	**Everard Cock**, born Wells, Somerset, 1890
Ewen	**Ewen Kerr**, baptized Inverness, Scotland, 15 January 1796

Fanny

The second and vulgar meaning has so overwhelmed the original that few children are now called Fanny. Little wonder, when it gave rise to name combinations such as these.

Fanny Action, baptized Claverley, Shropshire, 22 April 1747

Fanny Allbutt, born Lincoln, 1852

Fanny Beaver, born Bourne, Lincolnshire, 1839

Fanny Bendova, born Italy, c.1876 (New Haven, Connecticut, 1910 US census)

Fanny Biggadyke, baptized Whaplode, Lincolnshire, 24 May 1744

Fanny Bottom, born Derby, 1900

Fanny Bum, born Oxfordshire, c.1839 (Binfield, Oxfordshire, 1841 census)

Fanny Bush, married Francis Cox, Ringwood, Hampshire, 7 February 1824

Fanny Bushy, born Middlesex, c.1812 (Whitechapel, London, 1841 census). *She also had a daughter with the same name, born c.1833.*

Fanny Buster, born St Albans, Hertfordshire, c.1866 (St Albans, 1891 census)

Fanny Bythesea, born India, c.1847 (Bath, Somerset, 1881 census)

Fanny Chaffer, born Westhampnett, Sussex, 1864

Fanny Cleaver, baptized St Michael, Coventry, 8 June 1755. *A 'fanny cleaver' is a slang term for a large penis.*

Fanny Cockup, born Dartford, Kent, 1840

Fanny Comes, baptized Witton-cum-Twambrooks, Cheshire, 25 October 1857

Fanny Comewell, born Kings Norton, Leicestershire, c.1828 (Bournemouth, Hampshire, 1901 census)

Fanny Coming, born Crewe, Cheshire, c.1847 (Brackley St Peter, Northamptonshire, 1881 census)

Fanny Crack, born Barrow, Suffolk, c.1848 (Kingsbury, Middlesex, 1871 census)

Fanny Cream, married Robert Hardy, Eaton Socon, Bedfordshire, 13 August 1798

Fanny Creamer, born Pocklington, Yorkshire, 1872

Fanny Crevice, baptized Old Swinford, Worcestershire, 16 September 1838

Fanny Crotch, baptized St Martin at Palace, Norwich, Norfolk, 13 July 1624

Fanny Cucker, born Sutton, Surrey, c.1857 (Sutton, 1871 census)

Fanny Cunt, born Colchester, Essex, c.1839 (Hastings, East Sussex, 1891 census). *Fanny Cunt lived in the seaside resort of Hastings with a bunch of Cunts: her son Richard (one hopes otherwise, but must assume he was known as 'Dick Cunt') and her daughters Ella and Violet Cunt, all of whom were born in Cape Colony (South Africa), and their brother Alfred Cunt, born in New Zealand. Fanny is described as 'living on her own means' – presumably she had acquired her unfortunate surname through marriage and returned from the colonies with her four children, but apparently minus Mr Cunt.*

Fanny Dicking, baptized Helion Bumpstead, Essex, 17 February 1721

Fanny Dickwell, born Butterwick, Lincolnshire, c.1859 (Leake, Lincolnshire, 1861 census). *Fanny was the daughter of Willy Dickwell Sr and sister of Willy Dickwell Jr.*

Fanny Dribble, born Mile End, London, c.1836 (Bethnal Green, London, 1901 census)

Fanny Eater, born c.1816 (Hampstead, London, 1841 census). *She is possibly the same Fanny Eater who shows up in the 1860 US census, in Middleborough, Plymouth, Massachusetts, as born in England in c.1815. Could she have been driven to emigrate by jokes about her name?*

Fanny E. C. Lay, born South Carolina, *c.*1877 (Dogwood Neck, South Carolina, 1880 US census)

Fanny Fanny, baptized St Pancras, London, 1837

Fanny Farty, born Rock, Worcestershire, *c.*1842 (Tenbury, Worcestershire, 1861 census)

Fanny Feeling, born Hampshire, *c.*1801 (Northwood, Hampshire, 1841 census)

Fanny Filler, born St Olave, Southwark, London, 1892

Fanny Filling, born Horsham, Sussex, *c.*1832 (Lingfield, Surrey, 1901 census)

Fanny Finger, born Ide Hill, Kent, *c.*1859 (Blacklands, Sussex, 1891 census)

Fanny Fister, born Weymouth, Dorset, *c.*1859 (Parkstone, Dorset, 1891 census)

Fanny Flasher, married Victor Grenbaum, Humberside, Lincolnshire, 1920

Fanny Flow, born Newport, Isle of Wight, *c.*1844 (Chelsea, London, 1901 census)

Fanny Fuck, married Vite Epstein, Cooper, Missouri, USA, 20 November 1851

Fanny Fucker, born *c.*1872; passenger on *Lusitania*, Liverpool, England–New York, USA, arrived 28 March 1908

Fanny Gash, baptized Syston, Lincolnshire, 29 July 1838

Fanny Growcock, born Bourne, Lincolnshire, 1852

Fanny Gush, baptized Budleigh Salterton, Devon, 1 November 1871

Fanny Gussett, born Kenilworth, Warwickshire, *c.*1859 (Duddeston cum Nechells, Warwickshire, 1871 census)

Fanny Hair, born Texas, c.1882 (Marlow, Oklahoma, 1930 US census)

Fanny Hammer, born Wisconsin, c.1863 (Milwaukee, Wisconsin, 1900 US census)

Fanny Hardon, born Lancaster, Lancashire, c.1904 (Lancaster, 1911 census). *Fanny was the daughter of Minnie Hardon (born c.1868) and sister of another Minnie Hardon (born c.1902) and Norah Hardon (born c.1909).*

Fanny Honey, buried Padstow, Cornwall, 12 November 1891

Fanny Humper, born Clerkenwell, London, c.1842 (St Luke, Old Street, London, 1851 census)

Fanny Hunter, born Rye, Kent, 1838

Fanny Hustler, baptized Pudsey, Yorkshire, 18 December 1785

Fanny Jane Penis, born Gloucester, 1842

Fanny Juice, baptized St Margaret, Westminster, London, 12 March 1650

Fanny Kiss, died Epping, Essex, 1874

Fanny Lapper, born Shoreditch, London, 1841

Fanny Lapping, born 14 September 1888; died Pomona, California, USA, 30 October 1974

Fanny Lather, married Tonbridge, Kent, 1873

Fanny Licker, born Kentucky, 1885 (Louisville, Kentucky, 1900 US census)

Fanny Licking, born Leeds, Yorkshire, 1848

Fanny Lips, married John Christophers, Falmouth, Cornwall, 13 April 1823

Fanny Lovely, baptized Moulton, Lincolnshire, 10 October 1830

Fanny Lover, married Marylebone, London, 1850

Fanny Loving, born Isle of Wight, Hampshire, 1841

Fanny Lust, born Lewes, Sussex, 1844

Fanny May Leak, born Poplar, London, 1886

Fanny Merkin, born Thingoe, Suffolk, 1845

Fanny Minge, born Italy, c.1873 (Somerset, New Jersey, 1920 US census)

Fanny Minger, born South Carolina, c.1855 (Fairfield, South Carolina, 1870 US census)

Fanny Muff, born Leeds, Yorkshire, c.1846 (Wortley, Yorkshire, 1871 census)

Fanny Munch, born Ohio, c.1858 (Ballville, Ohio, 1880 US census)

Fanny Oral, born Campbell, Kentucky, USA, 8 January 1861

Fanny Organ, born Frome, Somerset, 1838

Fanny Party, born Cumberland, c.1813 (Wimbledon, Surrey, 1871 census)

Fanny Passage, born Sheerness, Kent, c.1865 (Gillingham, Kent, 1891 census)

Fanny Pie, married Robert Marsh, Wigan, Lancashire, 1923

Fanny Pimp, born Sleaford, Lincolnshire, 1876

Fanny Plenty, born Shoreditch, London, 1867

Fanny Poker, born Henley-on-Thames, Oxfordshire, c.1877 (Remenham, Berkshire, 1901 census)

Fanny Pounder, born Manchester, Lancashire, 1879

Fanny Pumper, born Mile End, London, c.1879 (St George in the East, London, 1881 census)

Fanny Pussey, born Yorkshire, c.1817 (Holderness, Yorkshire, 1841 census)

Fanny Quim, born Georgia, c.1855 (Schley, Georgia, 1870 US census)

Fanny Shafter, born Durham, c.1811 (Durham, 1841 census)

Fanny Shaggs, born Datchworth, Hertfordshire, c.1832 (Hertford, 1851 census)

Fanny Shaver, married Stockton-on-Tees, Durham, 1842

Fanny Softness, married Samuel Cohen, Mile End, London, 1925

Fanny Stretcher, born Gloucester, 1877

Fanny Stuffer, born Ohio, 1893 (Dayton, Ohio, 1900 US census)

Fanny Tickler, born Withern, Lincolnshire, c.1859 (Grimsby, 1881 census)

Fanny Tight, born Ware, Hertfordshire, 1857

Fanny Tongue, born West Bromwich, Staffordshire, 31 July 1881

Fanny Tush, born Hull, Yorkshire, c.1849 (Sculcoates, Yorkshire, 1871 census)

Fanny Wankman, born Colchester, Essex, c.1789 (Stepney, London, 1851 census)

Fanny Warmer, married Newent, Gloucestershire, 1875

Fanny Washer, married Axbridge, Somerset, 1846

Fanny Watmuff, born Bradford, Yorkshire, *c*.1863 (Cottingley, Yorkshire, 1871 census)

Fanny Wetnight, born Maryland, *c*.1855 (Middleton, Maryland, 1870 US census)

Fanny Wetter, born St Austell, Cornwall, 1846

Fanny Wide, married Cardiff, Glamorgan, 1900

Fanny Wig, born Hartley Wintney, Hampshire, 1838

Fanny Wonder, married Whitechapel, London, 1907

Fanny Worker, baptized Ridgmont, Bedfordshire, 6 June 1824

Fay   **Fay King**, born 1922; died Bromley, Kent, 1998

        Fay Mouse, born Kentucky, *c*.1906 (Liberty, Kentucky, 1920 US census)

Flint   **Flint Lock**, born Alabama, *c*.1908 (Houston, Alabama, 1930 US census)

        Flint Stone, baptized Marsham, Norfolk, 12 September 1790

Flo   **Flo Rider**, born 12 March 1923; died York, Pennsylvania, USA, 15 November 1998

Flossie   **Flossie Candy**, born Shepton Mallet, Somerset, *c*.1858 (Wincanton, Somerset, 1871 census)

Fran   **Fran Tick**, married Shoreditch, London, 1877

Frank   **Frank Furter**, born 3 August 1889; died Russellton, Pennsylvania, USA, June 1972

Fred   **Fred Egg**, born Lymington, Hampshire, 1858

Frida   **Frida Egg**, born 28 April 1861; married Albert Ernst, Thurgau, Switzerland, 28 October 1890

Gail   **Gail Force**, born Shoals, Indiana, USA, 20 September 1895

Gay *Linguistic change has resulted in the decline of once-popular Gay, which formerly produced rather exotic combinations.*	**Gay Barr**, born Illinois, c.1893 (Lake Creek, Williamson, Illinois, 1910 US census)
	Gay Beaver, born St Pancras, London, c.1897 (St Marylebone, London, 1901 census)
	Gay Bender, born Alabama, c.1861 (Georgiana, Alabama, 1930 US census)
	Gay Bird, born Indiana, c.1888 (Wabash, Indiana, 1930 US census)
	Gay Boy, born China, c.1891 (Kootenay, British Columbia, 1911 Canada census)
	Gay Lust, born 5 January 1909; died Spokane, Washington, USA, 9 March 1995
	Gay Ness, born c.1902 (Aux Sable, Illinois, 1930 US census)
	Gay Power, resident of Kalgoorlie, Western Australia, 1906 (1901–36 Australian electoral rolls)
	Gay Pride, born 16 April 1917; died Wandsworth, London, May 2003
Gene	**Gene Pool**, born Kentucky, c.1876 (Caneyville, Kentucky, 1930 US census)
George	**George Dragon**, born c.1698; baptized St Katherine Creechurch, London, 10 February 1704
	George Ia, born Oldbury, Worcestershire, c.1864 (Oldbury, 1891 census)
	George Porges, born Manchester, Lancashire, c.1869 (Pendlebury and Swinton, Lancashire, 1901 census)
Glad	**Glad Wragg**, born Bakewell, Derbyshire, 1894
Gladys	**Gladys Friday**, born 1900; died Brent, Middlesex, 1987
	Gladys Over, born Foleshill, Warwickshire, 1898

Grace	**Grace Less**, married William Gifford, Taunton, Somerset, 8 September 1738
Hans	**Hans Up**, born 15 April 1722; baptized Sodra Melby, Kristianstad, Sweden, 15 April 1722; died 4 February 1728
Harry *You may be just wild about Harry – it's the fourth most popular boy's name in England and Wales – but it's just too close for comfort to 'Hairy' in certain combinations.*	**Harry Balls**, married Thingoe, Suffolk, 1869
	Harry Balz, born Maryland, *c*.1865 (Baltimore, Maryland, 1870 US census)
	Harry Beaver, baptized St Mary Portsea, Hampshire, 21 November 1812
	Harry Bottom, baptized Holy Trinity, Rugby, Warwickshire, 6 January 1861
	Harry Bummy, born Liverpool, Lancashire, *c*.1873 (West Derby, Lancashire, 1901 census)
	Harry Chopper J. Percy, born Gravesend, Kent, 1879
	Harry Cunt, born Runcorn, Cheshire, *c*.1874 (mate on ship Thistle, Mersey, Lancashire, 1901 census). *As the captain claimed his name was Robert Ball, Harry (Hairy?) Cunt may possibly have been a joke played on a naïve census enumerator.*
	Harry Dyke, born Germany, *c*.1883 (Sausalito, California, 1910 US census)
	Harry Hole, born *c*.1843; passenger on *Neville*, London, England–Sydney, Australia, arrived 11 September 1862
	Harry Kunt, born *c*.1908; passenger on *Leviathan*, Halifax, Nova Scotia, Canada–New York, USA, arrived 27 July 1931
	Harry Minge, born Virginia, *c*.1835 (Faunsdale, Alabama, 1880 US census)
	Harry Muff, born Bradford, Yorkshire, 1857

Harry Nuts, born Maryland, *c*.1868 (Baltimore, Maryland, 1880 US census)

Harry Pussey, born Croydon, Surrey, *c*.1863 (Croydon, 1901 census)

Harry Sack, born Russia, *c*.1885 (Spotswood, New Jersey, 1920 US census)

Harry Schlong, born New York. *c*.1877 (New York, 1910 US census). *'Schlong' is Yiddish slang for penis.*

Harry Zona, born 26 August 1901; died Ellwood City, Pennsylvania, USA, May 1974

Hattie   **Hattie Bowler**, married F. M. Starring, Kootenai, Idaho, USA, 21 September 1910

Hattie Box, born Texas, *c*.1895 (Crockett, Texas, 1910 US census)

Hattie Coates, married Middlesbrough, Yorkshire, 1895

Hazel	**Hazel Nutt**, born Holborn, London, 1894
	Hazel Twig, born Indiana, *c.*1901 (Wabash, Indiana, 1910 US census)
Heidi	**Heidi High**, died Alachua, Florida, USA, 17 November 1979
Helen	**Helen Back**, born Tiverton, Devon, 1849
	Helen B. Merry, born Winchester, Hampshire, *c.*1891 (Falmouth, Cornwall, 1901 census)
Henrietta/ Henriette/ Henryetta *'Henry ate a...' is the obvious mishearing of this name.*	**Henrietta Bean**, married Henry Haveman, St Matthew, Bethnal Green, London, 19 September 1768
	Henrietta Cake, born 12 May 1820; baptized St Edmunds, Salisbury, Wiltshire, 29 May 1820
	Henrietta Cock, baptized Feock, Cornwall, 11 April 1830
	Henrietta Dick, born Birkenhead, Cheshire, 1900
	Henrietta Fanny, born Cheshire, *c.*1860 (St Martin, Cheshire, 1871 census)
	Henrietta Mosquito, born *c.*1884; died Toxteth Park, Lancashire, 1914
	Henrietta Peach, born Burton upon Trent, Staffordshire, 1875
	Henrietta Postman, born Scotland, *c.*1867 (Bootle, Lancashire, 1891 census)
	Henrietta Prick, born Liverpool, Lancashire, *c.*1845 (St Luke, London, 1871 census)
	Henrietta Waffle, born 7 February 1918; died Renton, Washington, USA, 18 November 2006
	Henrietta Willy, born New York, *c.*1832 (New York, 1850 US census)

Henriette Anus, married Jean Batiste Boulfrois, Saint-Aignan, France, 11 February 1738

Henryetta Pie, born South Carolina, c.1856 (Goethe, South Carolina, 1910 US census)

Hi/Hy[ram]   **Hi Noon**, born Radford, Nottinghamshire, 1878

Hy Geers, baptized Bridge Sollers, Herefordshire, 26 January 1681

Hy Wind, born Bethnal Green, London, c.1865 (Poplar, London, 1871 census)

Holly   **Holly Berry**, born Barnsley, Yorkshire, 1880

Holly Wood, born Faversham, Kent, 1901

Honour   **Honour Bound**, buried St Pinnock, Cornwall, 1783

Hugh(e)

Sorry, but Hugh is just too similar to 'huge', so why risk it if your surname gives rise to anything of this ilk?

Hugh Arse, born Saint Mary Steps, Exeter, Devon, 1701. *Arse was uncommon but not unknown as a surname in the sixteenth century: a John Arse (born c.1543) was recorded marrying a Marie Day in Rothley, Leicestershire, on 6 July 1568 – and how thrilled she must have been to find herself thenceforth known as 'Marie Arse'. From the seventeenth century we have a Dorothy Arse from Barnstaple, Devon, while in the eighteenth a whole family of Arses, probably of Spanish origin, resided in Milton Bryan, Bedfordshire, where Exequiel, son of Manuel Arse and Carmen Sagaseta, was baptized on 21 March 1877. His was the last Arse birth to be recorded, however, and by the time of the 1881 census, we find only an 'M. D. Arse', born in Germany in about 1855, a baker living in Holborn, London. The last of the British Arses had apparently all died of shame, changed their names, or perhaps emigrated to Bolivia, Mexico or Costa Rica where – numerically, at least – the Arses are much bigger.*

Hugh Belly, born Ireland, c.1801 (Liverpool, Lancashire, 1851 census)

Hugh Bollock, born New York, c.1877 (Brooklyn, New York, 1880 US census)

Hugh Boner, married Mary Silk, Baltimore, Maryland, USA, 12 August 1796

Hugh Bums, born Glasgow, Lanarkshire, c.1897 (Glasgow, 1901 Scotland census)

Hugh Cock, married Charlotte Over, Mevagissey, Cornwall, 19 June 1825

Hugh Dick, born Sheffield, Yorkshire, 1904

Hugh Dunnet, born Scotland, *c.*1836 ('attendant to the insane', Dinsdale Asylum, Dinsdale, Durham, 1861 census)

Hugh Fanny, born Staffordshire, *c.*1839 (Wolverhampton, Staffordshire, 1841 census)

Hugh Fatty, born Flint, *c.*1790 (Leadbrook Major, Flintshire, 1851 Wales census)

Hugh Janus, born *c.*1898; passenger on *Doric*, Liverpool, England–Quebec, Canada, arrived 17 August 1926

Hugh Jardon, born Virginia, *c.*1823 (Johnson, Ohio, 1870 US census).

Hugh Knicker, born Ireland, *c.*1866 (Maryhill, Lanarkshire, 1871 Scotland census)

Hugh Organ, born Port Glasgow, Renfrewshire, 18 June 1769

Hugh Penis Pritchard, born 1915; died Caernarfon, Gwynedd, 1990

Hugh Prick, born Shropshire, *c.*1801 (Oswestry, Shropshire, 1851 census)

Hugh Swelling, born Ireland, *c.*1811 (Kilbirnie, Ayrshire, 1851 Scotland census)

Hugh Tits, no date or place of birth given (Shamokin, Northumberland, Pennsylvania, 1830 US census)

Hugh Tool, born Cumberland, *c.*1850 (Wolsingham, Durham, 1881 census)

Hugh Wang, baptized St Oswald, Durham, 14 February 1568

Hugh Willy, baptized Old Kilpatrick, Dumbarton, 3 November 1743

Hughe Relief, born Stackpole Elidor, Pembrokeshire, *c.*1579

Ida

Ida Cock, married Jean Baptiste Paul Paquet, Paris, France, 22 September 1901. *Ida Cock was the daughter of Philomene Boobs.*

Ida Down, born Okehampton, Devon, 1894

Ida Ho, born New York, *c.*1877
(Buffalo, New York, 1880 US census)

Ima

Ima Badger, born 12 August 1934; died Woodland, California, USA, 9 February 2008

Ima Bird, born Iowa, *c.*1887
(Ouachita, Arkansas, 1910 US census)

Ima Box, born Missouri, *c.*1904
(Washburn, Missouri, 1920 US census)

Ima Cumming, born Michigan, *c.*1866
(Johnstown, Michigan, 1880 US census)

Ima Dick, born Missouri, *c.*1889
(Johnson, Oklahoma, 1920 US census)

Ima Fox, born Texas, 1894
(Bowie, Texas, 1900 US census)

Ima Gay, born Mississippi, *c.*1872
(Moscow, Mississippi, 1900 US census)

Ima Hogg, born 10 July 1882; died Houston, Texas, USA, 19 August 1975. *Ima Hogg was the daughter of James Hogg, the Governor of Texas. Her grandfather complained about her name, but too late – she had already been baptized. When she grew up, she signed her name with a scribble so that no one could read it. Some claim she had a sister called Ura Hogg, but this is an unfounded slur.*

Ima Hooker, born Texas, *c.*1896
(Rusk, Texas, 1910 US census)

Ima Hoover, born 17 February 1908; died Irene, Texas, USA, 13 July 1988

Ima Hore, born *c*.1896 (Durham, North Carolina, 1930 US census)

Ima Lady, born 19 June 1916; died Morris, Oklahoma, USA, 20 January 2005

Ima Looney, born Texas, *c*.1899 (Rusk, Texas, 1910 US census)

Ima Nutt, born *c*.1882 (Shelby, Texas, 1930 US census)

Ima Pain, born Georgia, 1891 (Clark, Georgia, 1900 US census)

Ima Pigg, born *c*.1890 (Erick, Oklahoma, 1930 US census)

Ima Rose Bush, born New York, *c*.1904 (Osceola, Michigan, 1910 US census)

Ima Smelly, born 14 July 1899; died Suwanee, Georgia, USA, June 1981

Ina   **Ina Box**, born Tennessee, *c*.1897 (Humphreys, Texas, 1910 US census)

Ina Hurry, born Arkansas, *c*.1907 (Texarkana, Arkansas, 1930 US census)

Iona   **Iona Dick**, born Ontario, 1888 (Saltcoats, Saskatchewan, 1911 Canada census)

Iona Gestring, born *c*.1902 (Kansas City, Kansas, 1930 US census)

Iris   **Iris Tew**, born 1922; died Chester and Ellesmere Port, Cheshire, 1985. *Her name arguably sounds like 'Irish stew' or 'Arrest you'.*

Isa   **Isa Wake**, born North Shields, Durham, *c*.1863 (Gateshead, Durham, 1891 census)

Isaac *Isaac or 'I suck...'?*

Isaac Balls, born Lexden, Essex, 1839

Isaac Beaver, born Pickering, Yorkshire, 1898

Isaac Dick, born Ohio, *c.*1854 (Cass, Ohio, 1880 US census)

Isaac Dicks, born New York, *c.*1793 (Poughkeepsie, New York, 1870 US census)

Isaac Hiscock, born Dorset, *c.*1831 (Tarrant Gunville, Dorset, 1841 census)

Isaac Hunt, baptized Bethersden, Kent, 29 June 1634. *He was the son of another Isaac Hunt.*

Isaac Mycock, son of Reuben Mycock, baptized Buxton, Derbyshire, 1876

Isaac Semen, married Caroline E. Hogan, St Clair, Illinois, USA, 19 January 1843

Isabel	**Isabel Ender**, born Perthshire, *c.*1796 (Alyth, Perthshire, 1841 Scotland census)
	Isabel Ringer, born Lambeth, London, *c.*1877 (Newington, London, 1881 census)
Isadora	**Isadora Wall**, born Clark, Ohio, *c.*1864 (Ohio, 1920 US census)
Isla	**Isla White**, born London, *c.*1846 (Aveley, Essex, 1851 census)
Iva *'I've thought* *of a name...'* *– but,* *unfortu-* *nately,* *it's Iva.*	**Iva Bump**, born Wisconsin, 1867 (Macon, Illinois, 1900 US census)
	Iva Cock, born Illinois, USA, *c.*1869 (South English, Iowa, 1925 Iowa state census)
	Iva Fanny, born Nebraska, *c.*1895 (Carnation, Washington, 1920 US census)
	Iva Ford, born Blything, Suffolk, 1882
	Iva Horn, born *c.*1882; passenger on *Berengaria*, New York, USA–Southampton, England, arrived 17 August 1927
	Iva Longbottom, born Balby, Yorkshire, *c.*1899 (Selby, Yorkshire, 1901 census)
	Iva Pain, born Missouri, *c.*1896 (Elsmore, Kansas, 1910 US census)
	Iva Pillow, born 2 June 1901; died Lake Elsinore, California, USA, 24 September 1982
	Iva Rash, born Kansas, USA, 23 May 1902; died San Bernardino, California, 10 June 1981
	Iva Reason, born 2 February 1876; died Farwell, Michigan, USA, March 1967
Ivan	**Ivan Anus**, born Saskatchewan, British Columbia, 1905 (Vancouver, British Columbia, 1911 Canada census)
	Ivan Austin, born Hastings, Sussex, 1883

Ivana	**Ivana Dick**, born c.1909 (Winterset, Iowa, 1930 US census)
Ivor	**Ivor Hardon**, born Llansamlet, Glamorgan, c.1878 (Swansea, Glamorgan, 1891 Wales census)
	Ivor Horn, born Cardiff, Glamorgan, 1907
	Ivor Million, died Derby, 1981
Ivy	**Ivy Holly**, born Eastbourne, Sussex, 1891
Izzy	**Izzy Gay**, born 12 May 1897; died Inverell, New South Wales, Australia, 3 October 1980
Jack	**Jack B. Quick**, born 19 March 1929; died Colorado Springs, Colorado, USA, 15 February 2008
	Jack Boot, born Uxbridge, Middlesex, 1899
	Jack Daw, born Bermondsey, London, c.1872 (Bermondsey, 1901 census)
	Jack Hoff, born Thetford, Norfolk, 1910
	Jack Off, married Sarah Clarke, St Peters, Thetford, Norfolk, 28 December 1773
	Jack Potts, born Wolstanton, Staffordshire, 1902
	Jack Schitz, born Germany, c.1893 (Bronx, New York, 1920 US census)
	Jack Spratt, born Epsom, Surrey, 1906
Jacob	**Jacob Slader**, born Devon, c.1796 (Tor Morham, Devon, 1841 census)
Jay	**Jay Walker**, born Battersea, London, c.1889 (Hackney, London, 1901 census)
Jean	**Jean Creamer**, born 29 June 1929; died Plymouth, Devon, March 1989
	Jean Jacket, born Ireland, c.1837 (Paisley, Renfrewshire, 1841 Scotland census)
	Jean Pool, born c.1841; died West Derby, Lancashire, 1899

Jennie/ Jenny	**Jennie Talia**, born c.1906 (Brooklyn, New York, 1930 US census)
	Jennie Talls, born Nebraska, 1899 (Douglas, Nebraska, 1900 US census)
	Jenny Talia Ferro, born Virginia, c.1857 (Massies, Nelson, Virginia, 1880 US census)
Jim/Jimmy	**Jim Locker**, married Stoke-on-Trent, Staffordshire, 1864
	Jim Shoe, married Bawdrip, Somerset, 28 February 1602
	Jim Slip, born Bath, Somerset, 1856
	Jimmy Riddle, born Melrose, Midlothian, 19 March 1648
Job	**Job Blower**, born Stockton, Shropshire, 27 August 1727
Joe	**Joe Blob**, born Wisconsin, c.1896 (Menasha, Wisconsin, 1930 US census). *A spoonerism if ever there was one.*
	Joe King, married Alice Adams, North Mimms, Hertfordshire, 15 April 1668

John Thomas

It is bad enough to be named after the coy euphemism used by Mellors, the gamekeeper in Lady Chatterley's Lover, for his penis, but when coupled with certain surnames it creates a double disaster.

John Thomas Cock, born c.1859; died Penzance, Cornwall, 1894. *He was one of at least twenty-three John Thomas Cocks born in the period 1837–1902.*

John Thomas Dong, born Bradford, Yorkshire, c.1868 (Bradford, 1901 census)

John Thomas Massage, married Maria Catharine Bond, Old Church, St Pancras, London, 17 June 1780

John Thomas Organ, born Newport, Monmouthshire, 1856

John Thomas Willy, baptized St George the Martyr, Southwark, London, 25 December 1812

Johnny	**Johnny B. Goode** (female), born Texas, c.1907 (Lee, Texas, 1910 US census)
Jonah	**Jonah Whalebelly**, born Saham Toney, Norfolk, c.1818 (Saham Toney, 1891 census)
Joss	**Joss Stick**, born Ulverston, Lancashire, 1887
Joy	**Joy Jolly**, born 21 February 1938; died Biggleswade, Bedfordshire, 1991
	Joy Rider (male), born Missouri, 1895 (Kansas City, Missouri, 1900 US census)
Juan	**Juan Afuck**, born c.1847; passenger on *Santiago*, Havana, Cuba–New York, USA, arrived 11 July 1883
	Juan King, born Mississippi, c.1904 (Franklin, Mississippi, 1920 US census)
	Juan P. Nis, baptized Blanchland, Northumberland, 30 April 1837
Juliet	**Juliet A. Cock**, born New York, 1852 (Oswego, New York, 1900 US census)
Justin	**Justin Case**, born New York, c.1832 (Bowne, Missouri, 1870 US census)
	Justin Pussy, married Marie Salleron, Paris, France, 2 May 1821
Kate	**Kate Grunt**, born Kansas, c.1879 (Homewood, Kansas, 1910 US census). *A fine example of a name spoonerism.*
Ken	**Ken Tuckey**, born 22 June 1916; died Naugatuck, Connecticut, USA, 30 April 1997
Kitty	**Kitty Litter**, born Martson, Cheshire, c.1839 (Wincham, Cheshire, 1851 census)
Laurie	**Laurie Driver**, born 1895; died Surrey, 1990
Lea	**Lea King**, born Chard, Somerset, c.1777 (North Wraxall, Wiltshire, 1861 census)
Len	**Len Tills**, born Stockton-on-Tees, Durham, 1905

Les	**Les Bean**, born Iowa, *c.*1864 (Lone Oak, Missouri, 1930 US census)
	Les Behan, born Iowa, *c.*1887 (Mohall, North Dakota, 1930 US census)
	Les Moore, born 1935; died Enfield, Middlesex, 2000
Lettice	**Lettice Agree**, born Mottram, Cheshire, *c.*1866 (Ashton-under-Lyne, Lancashire, 1871 census)
	Lettice Bray, baptized Mobberley, Cheshire, 26 April 1807
	Lettice Spray, baptized Greasley, Nottinghamshire, 23 April 1633
Levi	**Levi Jeans**, baptized Stalbridge, Dorset, 24 February 1811
Lew	**Lew Pole**, born Pontypridd, Glamorgan, 1898
	Lew Swires, born Pennsylvania, 1868 (Dean, Pennsylvania, 1900 US census)
Liz	**Liz Ard**, born Ireland, *c.*1824 (Waltham Abbey, Essex, 1871 census)
	Liz Bian, born Hertfordshire, *c.*1786 (Hitchin, Hertfordshire, 1841 census)
Liza	**Liza Wrong**, baptized St Margaret, Westminster, London, 11 February 1618
Lorna	**Lorna Mower**, born Utah, *c.*1906 (Fairview, Utah, 1910 US census)
Lot	**Lot Terry**, born Prestwich, Lancashire, 1884
Lotta	**Lotta Dick**, born France, *c.*1829 (Saint Louis, Missouri, 1880 US census)
	Lotta Luck, born Ontario, *c.*1882 (Oakville, Ontario, 1891 Canada census)
	Lotta Poo, married Hana Kalenahi, Hawaii, 15 February 1871
	Lotta Rump, born Flegg, Norfolk, 1902

Lou	**Lou Bricant**, born Pitton, Wiltshire, c.1807 (Pitton, 1871 census). *She also had a daughter of the same name.*
Lucky	**Lucky Day**, born Blything, Suffolk, 1859
Lucy	**Lucy Lube**, born Preston, Lancashire, c.1830 (Formby, Lancashire, 1881 census)
	Lucy Snatch, married Robert Colley, St Dunstan, Stepney, London, 11 June 1644
	Lucy Trunks, born Cardiff, Glamorgan, 1897
	Lucy Vagina, born Italy, 1887 (Alameda, California, 1900 US census)
Luke	**Luke Warm** (female), born Ely, Cambridgeshire, c.1891 (Ely, 1901 census)
Lulu	**Lulu Bonks**, born Illinois, 1877 (New York, 1900 US census)
Lydia	**Lydia Bin**, born Massachusetts, USA, c.1770; died Florida, Massachusetts, 1850
	Lydia Chutney, born Illinois, c.1861 (Okawville, Illinois, 1880 US census)
	Lydia Kettle, born Marylebone, London, 1839
Maggie	**Maggie Zine**, born Kensington, London, c.1871 (Willesden, Middlesex, 1891 census)
Marcia	**Marcia Mallow**, born Michigan, 1890 (Athens Village, Michigan, 1900 US census)
Margherita	**Margherita Pizza**, born Italy, c.1849; passenger on *Neckar*, Naples, Italy–New York, USA, arrived 2 June 1907
Maria	**Maria Entry**, born Publow, Somerset, c.1813 (Bedminster, Somerset, 1861 census)
	Maria Fuck, born Stolberg, Germany, 19 November 1890; died Epichnellen, 24 May 1945
	Maria Orefice, born Holborn, London, 1895

Marian	**Marian Haste**, died Fylde, Lancashire, 1947
Marjorie	**Marjorie Daw**, born Wandsworth, London, 1891
Martha	**Martha Rogers Mycock**, married Rotherham, Yorkshire, 1887
Mary	**Mary Hinge**, born Clutton, Somerset, 1846. *A spoonerism.*
	Mary Land, baptized Taynton, Gloucestershire, 2 February 1599
	Mary Lickcock, married Mike Warso, Mercer, Pennsylvania, USA, 28 June 1892
	Mary Lovesit, married Thomas Goldsmith, Trinity Church, New York, USA, 20 October 1784
	Mary Sanus, married Samuel Wilkinson, Birstall, Yorkshire, 29 July 1824
	Mary Sarse, born Holt, Worcestershire, *c.*1851 (Kempsey, Worcestershire, 1871 census)
	Mary Screws, married Edward Taylor, Canterbury, Kent, 2 January 1710
	Mary Xmas, baptized Petworth, Sussex, 10 December 1759
	Mary Zarse, born Cornwall, *c.*1811 (Mevagissey, Cornwall, 1841 census)
Matt	**Matt Black**, born Felling, Durham, *c.*1861 (Holmside, Durham, 1891 census)
Maude	**Maude Ship**, born London, *c.*1866 (Hackney, London, 1901 census). *She had a daughter, another Maude Ship, born c.1892.*
Max	**Max Power**, born Tredegar Park, Newport, Monmouthshire, *c.*1856 (Newport, 1881 Wales census)
	Max Speed, born Louth, Lincolnshire, 1861

May	**May B. Nott**, born Illinois, 1869 (Kewanne, Illinois, 1900 US census)
	May Bee, married James Rowlands, Scarborough, Yorkshire, 1922
	May Bumwell, born Indiana, c.1843 (Milford, Nebraska, 1870 US census)
	May Cheat, born Maine, c.1872 (Rockland, Maine, 1880 US census)
	May Day, died Axbridge, Somerset, 1842
	May Fair, born Nantwich, Cheshire, 1880. *The cockney pronunciation of 'Mayfair', one of London's smartest areas, gave rise to the title of the musical* My Fair Lady.
	May Fly Away, born 1896 (Fort Berthold, 1896 US Indian census)
	May Holiday, born Westminster, London, 1878
	May Igo, born Illinois, c.1861 (Chicago, Illinois, 1880 US census)
	May Pole, born Leicester, 1904
	May Wank, born Kirkee, India, c.1886 (Charlton, London, 1901 census)
Mel	**Mel Oddy**, born Halifax, Yorkshire, 1886
Mercy	**Mercy Mee**, born Loughborough, Leicestershire, 1880
Mich	**Mich Egan**, born Ireland, 1866 (Manhattan, New York, 1900 US census)
Mike	**Mike Hock**, born Wigan, Lancashire, 1892
	Mike Hunt, born Chippenham, Wiltshire, 1842
	Mike Robe, baptized Kilsyth, Stirling, 15 May 1743
	Mike Rotch, born Ireland, c.1817 (Stockport, Cheshire, 1861 census)
	Mike Stand, born Durham, c.1844 (Newcastle upon Tyne, Northumberland, 1851 census)

Miles	**Miles High**, born Ulverston, Cumberland, 1860
	Miles Long, born Sleaford, Lincolnshire, 2 January 1661
	Miles More, born Randwick, Gloucestershire, *c.*1824 (Standish, Gloucestershire, 1851 census)
	Miles O'Toole, born *c.*1839; died St Pancras, London, 1866
Millie	**Millie Peed**, died Lauramie Township, Indiana, USA, 10 December 1912

Min/Minnie	**Min Spiess**, born Laverton, Gloucestershire, c.1876 (Snowshill, Gloucestershire, 1891 census)
	Minnie Balls, born West Ham, Essex, 1870
	Minnie Ballsacker, mother of Ethel Louise Augusta Brinkmayer, born St Louis, Missouri, USA, 3 August 1908
	Minnie Bar, baptized Galston, Ayr, 25 June 1761
	Minnie Cock, born Nova Scotia, 24 December 1877 (Colchester, Nova Scotia, 1901 Canada census)
	Minnie Cooper, born Spalding, Lincolnshire, 1859
	Minnie Disque, married John Stoll, Hamilton, Ohio, USA, 22 June 1886
	Minnie Fart, born Martock, Somerset, c.1875 (Ravenstone with Snibston, Leicestershire, 1901 census)
	Minnie Mee, born Derby, 1873
	Minnie Minor, born Bristol, Gloucestershire, 1889
	Minnie Mouse Mollinson, born Chelsea, London, 1859
	Minnie Penis, born Mississippi, 1892 (Tate, Mississippi, 1900 US census)
	Minnie Skirt, baptized St Mary's, Sandwich, Kent, 17 July 1777
	Minnie Sowter, born Mansfield, Nottinghamshire, 1893
Mona	**Mona Lott**, born Germany, c.1845 (Galveston, Texas, 1850 US census)
Moses	**Moses Lawn**, born Ireland, c.1844 (Philadelphia, Pennsylvania, 1870 US census)

Nan	**Nan Tucket**, baptized Upton Pyne, Devon, 21 November 1790
Nancy	**Nancy Boy**, born Illinois, c.1819 (Sebastian, Arkansas, 1860 US census)
	Nancy Boys, born Brighton, Sussex, c.1842 (Brighton, 1871 census)
Neale	**Neale Down**, born 7 March 1823; baptized St Mary, St Marylebone Road, London, 2 April 1823
Nev	**Nev Ada** (female), born Kansas, c.1870 (Oklahoma, USA, 1890 Oklahoma census)

Nicholas
As illustrated by the old knock-knock joke, 'Nicholas' – 'Nicholas who?' – 'Knickerless girls shouldn't climb trees', you have to be a bit careful with this name.

Nicholas Orgy, baptized St Martin-in-the-Fields, London, 26 December 1626

Nicholas Streaker, baptized St Oswald, Durham, 27 October 1747

Nicholas Virgin, born Guisborough, Yorkshire, 1875

FREDK J. STAPLES. 279. HIGH STREET. CAMDEN TOWN.

Nick	**Nick Kerr**, born 5 July 1884; died Columbia, South Carolina, USA, January 1973
	Nick Money, born 22 November 1891; died Fort Recovery, Ohio, USA, December 1972
Noah	**Noah Lott**, baptized Hipswell, Yorkshire, 16 August 1843
	Noah Sark, born Indiana, c.1882 (Bartlesville, Oklahoma, 1902 US census)
	Noah Tall, baptized Antony, Cornwall, 21 April 1783
Noel	**Noel Plate**, born Binfield, Buckinghamshire, c.1847 (Hendon, Middlesex, 1891 census)
Nora(h)	**Nora Balls**, born Cratfield, Suffolk, c.1809 (Cratfield, 1891 census)
	Nora Bone, born South Stoneham, Hampshire, 1902
	Nora Bottom, born Ecclesall Bierlow, Yorkshire, 1905
	Nora Cock, born Greenwich, London, 1900
	Nora Dick, born Strickland Roger, Westmorland, c.1898 (Strickland Roger, 1901 census)
	Nora Fanny, born Grantham, Lincolnshire, c.1873 (Leyton, Essex, 1901 census)
	Nora Rawbone, born Kenysham, Somerset, 1904
	Norah Balls, born North Shields, Northumberland, c.1887 (Tynemouth, Northumberland, 1901 census)
Norma	**Norma Stitz**, born c.1824 (Benton, Indiana, 1930 US census)
Norman	**Norman Conquest**, born Lewisham, London, 1904
	Norman Knight, born Elland, Yorkshire, 15 August 1887

Olga	**Olga Flabbi**, born 20 December 1918; died Johnston City, Illinois, USA, March 1972
Olive	**Olive Branch**, born West Ham, Essex, 1880
Oliver	**Oliver Beer**, born Salisbury, Wiltshire, 1853
'Oliver' or 'I'll have a...?':	**Oliver Pancake**, born 4 November 1895; died Grosse Pointe, Michigan, USA, June 1975

Ophelia

'I feel your pain' is the obvious response to anyone saddled with these names.

Ophelia Ball, born Ashby-de-la-Zouch, Leicestershire, 1874

Ophelia Balls, born Georgia, c.1885 (Chatham, Georgia, 1910 US census)

Ophelia Beaver, born 17 February 1918; died Hico, West Virginia, USA, 15 February 2009

Ophelia Bristol, born Michigan, 1857 (Otisco, Ionia, Michigan, 1900 US census)

Ophelia Butt, born Tennessee, c.1879 (Maury, Tennessee, 1880 US census). *Ophelia Butt was the sister of Willy Butt.*

Ophelia Cock, born New York, c.1860 (New York, 1870 US census)

Ophelia Cocks, born Oxfordshire, c.1800 (St Marylebone, London, 1871 census)

Ophelia Cumming, born Georgia, c.1878 (Columbia, Georgia, 1880 US census)

Ophelia Dick, born Alabama, 1857 (Mobile, Alabama, 1900 US census)

Ophelia Fanny Hole, born Bristol, Gloucestershire, 1859

Ophelia Harden, born Louisiana, c.1890 (Hardy, Louisiana, 1920 US census)

Ophelia Kunz, born Georgia, c.1878 (Houston, Georgia, 1910 US census)

Ophelia Pubes, born Louisiana, c.1825 (Assumption, Louisiana, 1870 US census)

Ophelia Pusey, born Illinois, c.1866 (Condit, Illinois, 1870 USA census)

Ophelia Seaman, born New York, c.1833 (Reading, New York, 1860 US census)

Ophelia Self, born Louisiana, 1873 (Vernon, Louisiana, 1900 US census)

Ophelia Willy, born Mississippi, c.1902 (Alcorn, Mississippi, 1920 US census)

Orson	**Orson Carter**, born Llanelly, Monmouthshire, 1905
Oscar	**Oscar Queer**, born Pennsylvania, c.1885 (Derry, Pennsylvania, 1910 US census)
Owen	**Owen Money**, born Headington, Oxfordshire, 1884
Paddy	**Paddy Fields**, born West Derby, Lancashire, 1908
Page	**Page Turner**, born Axminster, Devon, 1865
Pansy(e)	**Pansy Blossom**, born Illinois, c.1896 (Macon, Illinois, 1910 US census)
	Pansy Daffodil Parcell, born South Stoneham, Hampshire, 1902
	Pansye Swallows, born 4 November 1909; died Fort Lauderdale, Florida, USA, 14 January 2001
Pat	**Pat Fenis**, born c.1875; passenger on *Celtic*, New York, USA–Liverpool, England, arrived 2 August 1913. *An unfortunate spoonerism of a name.*
	Pat Mycock, died Manchester, Lancashire, 1946
Patience	**Patience Mayhem**, married William Vigian, Maidstone, Kent, 19 January 1596
Pearl	**Pearl Button**, born Hollingbourne, Kent, 1903
	Pearl E. Gates, born 12 August 1899; died Lincoln, Iowa, USA, 26 April 1989
	Pearl E. White, born Gravesend, Kent, 1908
Pedor	**Pedor File** (male), born Glasgow, Lanarkshire, c.1864 (Barrhead, Renfrewshire, 1871 Scotland census)

Peg   **Peg Basket**, born Tennessee, *c.*1836
(Wilson, Tennessee, 1870 US census)

                Peg Legg, born Stuntney, Cambridgeshire,
*c.*1900 (Ely, Cambridgeshire, 1901 census)

Penny   **Penny Farthing**, born England, *c.*1815
(Gravesend, New York, 1860 US census)

                Penny Tent, licence to marry Nathaniel Crew,
2 December 1691

Pete(r)   **Pete Bog**, married Eliza Young, St Pancras,
London, 1812

                Pete Moss, baptized Acton by Nantwich,
Cheshire, 22 June 1679

                Pete Sake, born Cheshire, *c.*1840
(Macclesfield, Cheshire, 1841 census)

                Peter Eater, born Pennsylvania, *c.*1868
(Lower Allen, Pennsylvania, 1920 US census)

                Peter Upass, born Mexico, *c.*1866
(Jackson, Louisiana, 1910 US census)

Phil/Phila	**Phil (Philomene) A. Tio**, born c.1862; married William P. Rideau, New Orleans, Louisiana, USA, 12 November 1883
	Phil Ander, born Westminster, London, c.1842 (St Martin-in-the-Fields, London, 1871 census)
	Phil Attele, born Germany, c.1817 (Chicago, Illinois, 1850 US census)
	Phil Bins, born Ohio, c.1848 (Clay, Ohio, 1850 US census)
	Phil Fanny, born Gorton, Lancashire, c.1800 (Gorton, 1851 census)
	Phil Gapp, married Forehoe, Norfolk, 1859
	Phil Graves, died Rotherham, Yorkshire, 1879
	Phil Harrup, born Royston, Hertfordshire, 1839
	Phil Lander, born Stoke Damerel, Devon, 1846
	Phil Ling, born St Olave, Southwark, London, 1882
	Phil McCracken, born Lewisham, Kent, c.1877 (Lewisham, 1911 census)
	Phil Rupp, born France, c.1897 (Lander, Wyoming, 1920 US census)
	Phila Delphia, born Cornwall, 1840 (Buryan, Penwith, Cornwall, 1841 census)
Phillip	**Phillip Ines**, born c.1821 (St Paul, Covent Garden, London, 1841 census)
Phyllis	**Phyllis Hole**, born Greenwich, London, 1906
	Phyllis Private Holes, born Eastbourne, Sussex, 1893
Pierce	**Pierce Deare**, married Elizabeth Portman, St Gregory by Paul's, London, 14 April 1635

Pleasant	**Pleasant Fuck**, born Missouri, c.1859 (Blackwater, Pettis, Missouri, 1870 US census)
	Pleasant Pee, born Redgrave, Suffolk, c.1811 (Greenwich, Kent, 1871 census)
	Pleasant Titty, baptized St John, Margate, Kent, 3 April 1768. *She was named after her mother, so there was a pair of Pleasant Tittys in the family.*
Polly	**Polly Esther**, born Bradford, Yorkshire, c.1870 (Manningham, Yorkshire, 1871 census)
	Polly Parrot, baptized Luddington, Lincolnshire, 21 June 1778
	Polly Tickle, born Clifton, Lancashire, c.1876 (Swinton, Lancashire, 1901 census)
Precious	**Precious Little**, born 14 June 1944; died Los Angeles, California, USA, 6 January 1982
Randy	**Randy Beaver** (female), born Pennsylvania, c.1897 (Middle Smithfield, Pennsylvania, 1910 US census)
	Randy Bumgardner, born Ohio, USA, 9 July 1975; died 29 November 2004
	Randy Dick, born 4 February 1970; died Monticello, Kentucky, USA, 3 October 2008
	Randy Dyke, born Alderbury, Wiltshire, 1886
	Randy Guest, born Sussex, c.1795 (Wadhurst, Sussex, 1841 census)
	Randy Midgett, born North Carolina, c.1876 (Alligator, North Carolina, 1880 US census)
	Randy Rimmer, born 6 October 1962; died Iredell, North Carolina, USA, February 1986

Ray	**Ray Gunn**, born 3 August 1930; died Orlando, Florida, USA, 12 December 1988
	Ray Zerr, born 7 January 1928; died Albany, Oregon, USA, June 1978
Rhoda	**Rhoda Boat**, born Rogate, Hampshire, c.1813 (Graffham, Sussex, 1861 census)
	Rhoda Broom, baptized St Matthew, Walsall, Staffordshire, 7 September 1795
	Rhoda Cock, married Thomas Lovack, South Lopham, Norfolk, 9 February 1815
	Rhoda Cunt, born Tennessee, c.1863 (Tennessee, 1870 US census)
	Rhoda Duck, born Guisborough, Yorkshire, 1905
	Rhoda Dyke, born Pewsey, Wiltshire, 1869
	Rhoda Fanny, born Widnes, Lancashire, c.1876 (Eccleston, Lancashire, 1891 census)
	Rhoda Fishback, born Louisiana, c.1875 (Burke, Louisiana, 1920 US census)
	Rhoda Goodsheep, married Dudley, Staffordshire, 1874
	Rhoda I. Land, born Alabama, c.1868 (Choctaw, Mississippi, 1870 US census)
	Rhoda Penis, born Tennessee, c.1879 (Sullivan, Tennessee, 1880 US census)
Rick	**Rick O'Shea**, married Kennington, London, 1864
	Rick Shaw, born Romford, Essex, c.1857 (Tottenham, London, 1881 census)
Rob	**Rob Bery**, born Whitechapel, London, 1857
Robin	**Robin Banks**, born Denton, Lancashire, c.1864 (Denton, 1901 census)

Roger(s)

From Roger Moore to 'Roger and out', the obvious sexual association of Roger makes it a dicey first name that has given rise, as it were, to innumerable combinations along these lines.

Roger Dicks Moore, married East London, 1852

Roger Mee, died Bolton, Lancashire, 1856

Roger Mycock, born 31 October 1913; died King's Lynn, Norfolk, July 1997

Roger Myring, convicted Stafford, 26 February 1801; transported on *Glatton* to New South Wales, Australia, 1802–03

Roger Rimmer, baptized St Botolph, Aldgate, London, 30 May 1658

Roger Roger, baptized Moreton, Shropshire, 7 February 1587

Rogers Boys, born Newport, Monmouthshire, c.1848 (Newton Abbot, Devon, 1901 census)

Roland

Roland Butter, born Pennsylvania, c.1862 (Boggs, Pennsylvania, 1870 US census)

Rose/Rosie

Rose Bum, born Shoreditch, London, c.1891 (St Mary Stratford, Bow, London, 1901 census)

Rose Bush, born Shoreditch, London, 1864

Rose Humps, born Essex, c.1889 (Southend-on-Sea, Essex, 1911 census)

Rose Upward, born Iwerne, Dorset, c.1847 (Motcombe, Dorset, 1871 census)

Rosie Cheek, born Grays, Essex, c.1897 (Grays, 1901 census)

Rosetta	**Rosetta Cock**, married Stoke Damerel, Devon, 1888
Like Henrietta, above, 'Rose ate a...' can be heard in names such as these.	**Rosetta Dick**, born Illinois, *c.*1856 (Hamilton, Iowa, 1870 US census)
	Rosetta Gooseberry, born 9 October 1921; died New Orleans, Louisiana, USA, 6 August 2004
	Rosetta Nipple, born Ohio, *c.*1838 (Decatur, Green, Wisconsin, 1850 US census); married Green County, Wisconsin, 10 August 1862
	Rosetta Peniss, born Kensington, London, 1867
	Rosetta Stone, baptized St Giles without Cripplegate, London, 3 August 1828. *The Rosetta Stone was acquired by the British Museum in 1802.*
	Rosetta Viper, born Bishop's Stortford, Hertfordshire, 1862
Ruby	**Ruby Lips**, born Missouri, *c.*1900 (Marie, North Dakota, 1910 US census)
Rusty	**Rusty Pipes**, born 23 April 1975; died Missouri, USA, 26 May 1995
Sal	**Sal Monella**, born 1914; died Crawley, West Sussex, 1991
Sally	**Sally Mander**, born Maryland, *c.*1878 (Masseys, Maryland, 1880 US census)
Sandy	**Sandy Beach**, born St George in the East, London, *c.*1899 (St George in the East, 1901 census)
	Sandy Dune, born 23 December 1952; died Barstow, California, USA, 4 September 2000
Sarah	**Sarah Desert**, baptized St Leonard, Shoreditch, London, 1 April 1804
	Sarah Swallows, married John Wass, Fishlake, Yorkshire, 1733
	Sarah Tonin, married Thomas Clark, St Dunstan, Stepney, London, 1813

Scot(t)	**Scot Land**, born Kentucky, *c.*1891 (Butler, Ohio, 1920 US census)
	Scott Free, born Bethnal Green, London, 1901
Selby	**Selby Day**, born Ashton-under-Lyne, Lancashire, 1897
Seymour *'See more...' is inherent in names such as these classics.*	**Seymour Bust**, born Halstead, Essex, 1841
	Seymour Butt, born Bath, Somerset, 1875
	Seymour Pussy, baptized St Laurence, Catsfield, Sussex, 18 June 1836

Shawn	**Shawn Bush**, died Fort Worth, Texas, USA, 3 May 2007
Shirley	**Shirley Knott**, born Edmonton, Middlesex, 1902
Solomon	**Solomon Mines**, married Bath, Somerset, 1874. *H. Rider Haggard's popular adventure novel* King Solomon's Mines *was not published until 1885.*
Stan	**Stan Still**, born Malling, Kent, 1901
Sue	**Sue Age**, born Glasgow, Lanarkshire, c.1849 (Glasgow, 1851 Scotland census)
	Sue Flay, born Wellington, Somerset, 1871
	Sue Perman, born Wiltshire, c.1791 (Downton, Wiltshire, 1841 census)
	Sue Perrior, married David Yeatman, Downton, Wiltshire, 6 October 1755
	Sue Wage, born Wensey, Wiltshire, c.1839 (Lewisham, London, 1891 census)
	Sue You, born Saint Helena, c.1862 (British subject aboard Royal Navy ship *Flora*, Ascension, 1881 census)
Sydney	**Sydney Harbour**, born Chesterfield, Derbyshire, 1909
Tamara	**Tamara Knight**, born c.1882; died Aston, Warwickshire, 1892
Ted/Teddy	**Ted Ebear**, born Kent, Ontario, Canada, 8 August 1907
	Teddy Bear, born 1912; died Maidstone, Kent, 1998
	Teddy Boy, born St Giles, London, 1902
Tess	**Tess Tickle**, born Little Rock, Arkansas, USA, c.1893; married John H. Tickle; died Fort McPherson, Fulton, Georgia, 29 December 1923

Theresa	**Theresa Green**, baptized Motcombe, Dorset, 23 September 1804
Tim	**Tim Burr**, born Watford, Hertfordshire, 1867
Tina	**Tina Salmon**, born 8 November 1905; died Uvale, Texas, USA, 3 January 1984
Tom/ Tommy	**Tom A. Hawk**, born St Dennis, Cornwall, c.1890 (St Dennis, 1891 census)
	Tom Ato, born Sleaford, Lincolnshire, 1867
	Tom Bola, born Sheffield, Yorkshire, c.1841 (Sheffield, 1851 census)
	Tom Cat, baptized St Michael's, Withyham, Sussex, 16 October 1624
	Tom Tom, born Bristol, Gloucestershire, c.1862 (Barton Regis, Gloucestershire, 1891 census)
	Tommy Gun, born Evesham, Worcestershire, 1838
	Tommy Rot, born Shoreditch, London, 1871
Topsy	**Topsy Hatter**, born Rye, East Sussex, 1898
	Topsy Sharp, born Bristol, Gloucestershire, 1862. *Were her parents perhaps musically inclined, with 'Top C sharp' in mind?*
Ura	**Ura Buffalo**, born 5 April 1909; died Jacksonville, Texas, USA, 17 June 1994
	Ura Dick, born 17 February 1890; died Yonkers, New York, USA, 1976. *Ura was the mother of Rubin Dick.*
Valentine	**Valentine Card**, born 1913; died Chelmsford, Essex, 1993
	Valentine Day, born Leeds, Yorkshire, 1842
Vera	**Vera Boring**, born Alabama, c.1908 (Thompson, Alabama, 1910 US census)
	Vera Necessary, born 31 August 1922; died Tyler, Texas, USA, 19 November 2001

Vic	**Vic Tory**, born Bedford, 1908
Victoria	**Victoria Line**, died Birmingham, Warwickshire, 1960
	Victoria Station, born North Carolina, c.1842 (Edgecombe, North Carolina, 1870 US census)
Violet	**Violet Bum**, born Birmingham, Warwickshire, c.1897 (Aston, Warwickshire, 1901 census)
	Violet Cock, born St Austell, Cornwall, 1892
	Violet Corpse, born Whitby, Yorkshire, 1891
	Violet Minnie Balls, born St Pancras, London, 1896
	Violet Sandals, born Defford, Worcestershire, c.1886 (Cheltenham, Gloucestershire, 1911 census)
Walter	**Walter Cress**, married Sarah Wilton, St Mary the Virgin, Dover, Kent, 21 May 1805
	Walter Mellon, born Salford, Lancashire, 1839
	Walter Wall, born Witney, Oxfordshire, 1840
Wan	**Wan King**, born Delaware, c.1825 (Wilson, Illinois, 1860 US census)
Wanda	**Wanda Farr**, born Indiana, c.1904 (Indianapolis, Indiana, 1910 US census)
Wang	**Wang King**, born 15 October 1904; died New York, USA, 18 April 2001
Warren	**Warren Peace**, born New York, c.1866 (Essex, New York, 1880 US census)
Wayne	**Wayne Kerr**, born 28 November 1897; died Ozark, Arkansas, USA, February 1985
	Wayne Manger, born Pennsylvania, c.1877 (Reading, Pennsylvania, 1910 US census)
Wendy	**Wendy House**, died Texas, USA, 21 March 2005

Will/
William/
Willie/
Willy
Although
one of
the most
common
male first
names on
both sides
of the
Atlantic,
William's
shortened
forms
'Willie'
and 'Willy'
inevitably
produce
some un-
foreseen
combina-
tions.

Will Bumass, born Birmingham, Warwickshire, *c*.1892 (Birmingham, 1901 census)

Will Drown, born Vermont, *c*.1875 (Lyndon, Vermont, 1880 US census)

Will Ejack, born Pennsylvania, *c*.1886 (Pittsburgh, Pennsylvania, 1910 US census)

Will Fail, born Texas, USA, 25 April 1893 (World War I draft registration)

Will Fillerup, born Illinois, USA, *c*.1878 (Leon, Iowa, 1895 Iowa state census)

Will Gofar, baptized Howden, Yorkshire, 15 January 1632

Will Icome, born Whitechapel, London, 1856

Will Passwater, born New Jersey, *c*.1901 (Camden, New Jersey, 1910 US census)

Will Power, baptized Rye, Sussex, 27 February 1545

Will Ting, born Aldgate, London, *c*.1838 (City of London, 1891 census)

William A. S. Hole, born Burton upon Trent, Staffordshire, *c*.1887 (Buckhurst Hill, Essex, 1901 census)

William Job Blow, born Lincoln, 1887

Willie Dangle, born Pennsylvania, 1887 (Eldred, Pennsylvania, 1900 US census)

Willie Fister, born Brandon, Durham, *c*.1896 (Brandon, 1901 census)

Willie Gothard, born Alabama, *c*.1875 (Randolph, Alabama, 1910 US census)

Willie Harriet Wank, born Leytonstone, Essex, *c*.1868 (Wanstead, Essex, 1871 census). *To compound the embarrassment of his surname, Willie Wank received his mother's first name as his middle name.*

Willie Stretch, born Winsford, Cheshire, c.1894 (Chadderton, Lancashire, 1901 census)

Willie Sucking, born Elham, Kent, 1882

Willie Wanking, born c.1876 (Freshwater, Isle of Wight, 1911 census)

Willy Beatoff, born Somerset, c.1821 (Yeovil, Somerset, 1841 census)

Willy Dickus, born Ohio, c.1828 (Perry, Ohio, 1850 US census)

Willy Droop, resident of Kennedy, Queensland, 1905 (1901–36 Australian electoral rolls)

Willy Fokus, born Illinois, c.1896 (O'Fallon, Illinois, 1930 US census)

Willy Fucker, married Rosetta Yoakum, Caldwell, Missouri, USA, 2 January 1901

Willy Harddick, born 1867 (Halfmoon, Saratoga, New York, 1900 US census)

Willy Hugh Balls, born Kensington, London, 1874

Willy Inass, born Inverness, c.1835 (Inverness, 1861 Scotland census)

Willy Leak, married Marjorie Homer, Rowley Regis, Staffordshire, 1 December 1576

Willy Long (female), born Luton, Bedfordshire, c.1896 (Luton, 1901 census)

Willy Longcock, born 1833 (Lambeth, London, 1861 census)

Willy Orally, born Massachusetts, c.1869 (Medway, Massachusetts, 1870 US census)

Willy Semen, born Stirling, c.1854 (Stirling, 1871 Scotland census)

Willy Spunk, born Buxhall, Suffolk, c.1810 (Combs, Suffolk, 1881 census)

Willy Stroker, died Salford, Lancashire, 1872

Willy Sucker, born Germany, *c.*1907; crew on *Hansa*, Hamburg, Germany–New York, USA, arrived 2 July 1936

Willy Suckwell, baptized Asthall, Oxfordshire, 17 June 1838

Willy Wanker, born Angus, Scotland, *c.*1806 (Dundee, 1841 Scotland census)

Willy Wankoff, born Russia, *c.*1874 (Baltimore, Maryland, 1910 US census)

Win   **Win Dow**, born Maldon, Essex, 1886

Win King, born Lancashire, *c.*1839 (Manchester, Lancashire, 1841 census)

Win Wynn, born Prescot, Lancashire, 1889

A Catalogue of the Weird & Wonderful

Ill-conceived

As Humphrey Bogart says in *Casablanca*, 'We'll always have Paris.' He meant his and Ingrid Bergman's characters' fond memories of their time together in the world's most romantic capital, rather than someone called Paris – but he could have been predicting the future: from 1837 to 1915 in England and Wales just 165 babies were called Paris, whereas, influenced by the ubiquitous Paris Hilton, there have been almost 10,000 in the past decade – although a decline is evident, with only 135 girls (and five unfortunate boys) so called in 2008. It is rumoured that the trend-setter's name was derived from her place of conception, so it is fortunate that her parents did not spend the night in their Heathrow establishment. Actor-director Ron Howard added the place of conception as the middle name of all his children, hence Bryce Dallas Howard, Page Carlyle and Jocelyn Carlyle (named after the New York Carlyle hotel) Howard, and Reed Cross (apparently after a road – too much information, Ron) Howard. The Beckhams did it with Brooklyn, and the Clintons with Chelsea – but is this such a good idea?

Ashford	**Ashford Squirts**, born Wellow, Nottinghamshire, *c.*1851 (Greasley, Nottinghamshire, 1871 census)
Belfast	**Belfast Scott**, born Glasgow, *c.*1868 (Glasgow, 1871 Scotland census)
Birmingham	**Birmingham Bidgood**, born Taunton, Devon, 1849
Blackpool	**Blackpool Lovett**, born Rye, Sussex, *c.*1869 (Lowestoft, Suffolk, 1891 census)
Bognor	**Bognor Istran**, passenger on *Furnessia*, Valparaiso, Chile–Liverpool, UK, arrived 7 January 1907
Brighton	**Brighton Gay**, married Helston, Cornwall, 1881
Brixton	**Brixton Simmons**, born Brixton, London, *c.*1887 (Kensington, London, 1901 census)
Cairo	**Cairo Bender**, born 26 December 1898; died Wayne, Indiana, USA, 15 May 1966
Chelmsford	**Chelmsford Briscoe**, born Elmley Lovett, Worcestershire, *c.*1883 (Doddershill, Worcestershire, 1881 census)
Doncaster	**Doncaster Blyton**, born Market Raisen, Lincolnshire, *c.*1851 (Ollerton, Nottinghamshire, 1861 census)
Dunstable	**Dunstable McCarthy**, born Avon, Somerset, 1909
Eiffel Tower	**Eiffel Tower Sutherland**, born Indiana, *c.*1895 (Marion, Indiana, 1920 US census)
Grimsby	**Grimsby Poor**, born Ohio, *c.*1828 (Bloomfield, Ohio, 1870 US census)
Hackney	**Hackney Peacock**, born North Carolina, *c.*1897 (Nahunta, North Carolina, 1910 US census)

Hull	**Hull Chapman**, born Stainland, Yorkshire, c.1847 (Lindley Cum Quarmby, Yorkshire, 1881 census)
Hyde Park	**Hyde Park**, died Kensington, London, 1864
Liverpool	**Liverpool Kate**, died Manchester, Lancashire, 1905
London	**London Bridge**, born North Carolina, c.1848 (Jefferson, Missouri, 1870 US census)
	London England, born 26 January 1914; died Troy, Michigan, USA, 9 November 1989
Luton	**Luton Fawcett**, born Yorkshire, 1852
Paris	**Paris France**, born Missouri, c.1892 (Clark, Missouri, 1910 US census)
	Paris Harris, born 3 October 1898; died Kansas City, Missouri, USA, May 1972
Rotherham	**Rotherham Pilkington**, born Chesterfield, Derbyshire, 1851
Scunthorpe	**Robert Scunthorpe Free**, born Wisbech, Cambridgeshire, 1906
Slough	**Slough Robertson**, baptized St Peter's Chester, Cheshire, 20 June 1714
Stockport	**Stockport Higham**, born Stockport, Cheshire, 1854

'I am not a number...'*

We are familiar with the American habit of appending a number to a name, in the style of Fleetus Lee Gobble III (born 27 September 1947; died Winston Salem, North Carolina, USA, 30 June 1993), but it is hard to fathom the thinking of parents who opt to dispense with the name altogether and give their baby a number but many have done so. Is it an aide-mémoire to recalling the sequence of one's offspring? The commemoration of a lottery win? Sheer desperation?

Zero	**Zero Queen**, born Cleveland, North Carolina, USA, 10 September 1888; died Elbert, West Virginia, 9 April 1954
Tenth	**Tenth Lily West**, baptized Bedminster, Somerset, 22 June 1880
Eighth	**Eighth Hendricks**, born Texas, c.1909 (Robertson, Texas, 1910 US census)
Fifth	**Fifth Jesse**, born 14 November 1909; died Sacramento, California, USA, 16 March 1999
Quarter	**Quarter Harris**, baptized St Andrew Holborn, London, 1 May 1823
Half	**Half Robinson**, born Banbury, Oxfordshire, 1859
No. 1	**William No. 1 Harris**, married Islington, London, 1896
No. 2	**William No. 2 Harris**, married Maria A. Trent, Islington, London, 1913
Two	**Harry Two Smith**, married Derby, Derbyshire, 1900

* *The Prisoner* TV series, 1967–8 and 2010–

Three	**Three Worthy**, born 1 June 1907; died Linden, Alabama, USA, April 1981
Four	**Four Souls**, born 16 April 1907; died Box Elder, Montana, USA, July 1984
Five	**Five Bumball**, born Pennsylvania, c.1840 (Jackson, Missouri, 1920 US census)
Six	**Six Hix**, born South Carolina, c.1898 (Waterloo, South Carolina, 1910 US census)
Number Seven	**Number Seven Fell**, born Alton, Hampshire, 1879
Eight	**Eight McClurg**, born Iowa, c.1879 (White Breast, Iowa, 1880 US census)
Nine	**Nine Sparks**, born 18 July 1939; died Jackson, Montana, USA, 25 August 1995
Ten	**Ten Hipkiss**, born Birmingham, Warwickshire, c.1898 (Birmingham, 1911 Census)
Eleven	**Eleven Moore**, born 11 July 1900; died Coalgate, Oklahoma, USA, January 1982
Twelve	**Twelve Ripley**, born Illinois, 1887 (Ora, Illinois, 1900 US census)
Thirteen	**Thirteen Sneed**, born Tennessee, c.1882 (Tipton, Tennessee, 1920 US census)
Fourteen	**Fourteen Balm**, born Kentucky, c.1876 (Pulaski, Kentucky, 1920 US census)
Fifteen	**Fifteen Walker**, born South Carolina, c.1900 (Santee, South Carolina, 1920 US census)
Sixteen	**Sixteen Valentine**, born Texas, 1892 (Bowie, Texas, 1900 US census)
Seventeen	**Seventeen Banks**, born Texas, c.1873 (Lamar, Texas, 1880 US census)

Eighteen	**Eighteen Baker**, born Kentucky, 1876 (Louisville, Kentucky, 1900 US census)
Nineteen	**Ninteen Plomason**, born Minnesota, 1900 (Luverne, Minnesota, 1900 US census)
Twenty	**Twenty Hall**, born Fulham, London, 1859 (Fulham, 1861 census)
Thirty	**Thirty Wilson**, born Tennessee, c.1879 (Henry, Tennessee, 1880 US census)
Forty	**Forty Weieze**, born Germany, c.1858 (Willesden, Middlesex, 1901 Census)
Fifty	**Fifty Townsend**, born Alabama, c.1877 (Montgomery, Alabama, 1920 US census)
Fifty Six	**Fifty Six Richardson**, born Alabama, c.1869 (Gainesville, Alabama, 1870 US census)
Fifty Nine	**Tom Fifty Nine Contes**, born Darlington, Durham, c.1876 (Darlington, 1881 Census)
Sixty	**Sixty Moore**, born 1 July 1881; died Alaska, USA, December 1963
Seventy	**Seventy Head**, born 24 March 1897; died Pinellas, Florida, USA, July 1964
Eighty	**Eighty Coonrod**, born South Carolina, c.1843 (York, South Carolina, 1870 US census)
Ninety	**Ninety Griffin**, born 19 April 1908; died Apple Springs, Texas, USA, December 1980
Hundred	**Hundred Evans**, died Greene, Alabama, USA, 1 January 1949
Thousand	**Thousand Poindexter**, born Louisiana, c.1888 (Gibson, Louisiana, 1920 US census)

155. 'I am not a number...'

Million	**Million Airth**, born Ontario, Canada, 4 June 1869
Ten Million	**Ten Million**, born 14 October 1889; died Washington, USA, June 1964
Billion	**Billion Pride**, born c.1898 (Brooklyn, New York, 1930 US census)
Milliard	**Milliard Body**, born Birmingham, Warwickshire, c.1898 (Aston, Warwickshire, 1901 census). *A milliard is a synonym for a billion.*
Trillion	**Trillion Cummings**, born Mississippi, c.1907 (Kirkville, Mississippi, 1910 US census)
Quadrillion	**Quadrillion Christopher Jer** [sic] **Brown Jr**, died California, USA, 12 December 2008
Quintillion	**Quintillion Acock**, born Missouri, c.1856 (Looney, Missouri, 1870 US census)
Octillion	**Octillion Weed**, born Michigan, 1899 (Norwood, Michigan, 1900 US census)
Decillion	**Decillion Tate**, died Beaver, West Virginia, USA, 30 January 2007
Zillion	**Zillion Long**, born 15 March 1899; died Petersburg, Virginia, USA, October 1977. *Along with words such as squillion and gazillion, there is no such figure as a zillion, but it is sometimes used to mean a very large number.*
Infinity	**Infinity Hubbard**, born Georgia , c.1839 (Tippah, Mississippi, 1850 US census)

Driven Crazy

Many of these names anticipated those of the cars and related motoring items that they evoke, but in recent years a remarkable number of babies have received names that either celebrate the family runabout or could even be – though probably best not to go there – the place of conception. Some are perhaps aspirational – hence the large number of upmarket marques, most notably Porsche, including specific models such as the Porsche Carrera, and Mercedes, itself derived from the name of Mercédès Jellinek (1899–1929), the daughter of Daimler financier Emil Jellinek. Some car names are either commonplace (Toyota is a popular first name in Japan, while Riley, though defunct as a make of car, is the thirty-sixth most common boy's name in England and Wales, with Austin, Morgan and Morris still making an appearance). Some names, such as Volvo, have proved elusive, and while there is a Minnie Cooper, no Mini Cooper has come to light, nor, saddest of all, a Hertz Van Rental.

Allegro	**Allegro Manuel**, born 28 September 1905; died Franklin, Indiana, USA, April 1978
Aston Martin	**Aston Martin**, born 20 October 1912; died Dover, Delaware, USA, August 1970
Astra	**Astra Price**, born Quebec, Canada, c.1847 (Plymouth, Devon, 1891 census)
Audi	**Audi Lucas**, born 8 February 1891; died Beattyville, Kentucky, USA, November 1971
Austin	**Austin Driver**, born Saffron Walden, Essex, 1864

Auto	**Auto Riley**, born Alabama, c.1883 (Covington, Alabama, 1920 US census)
Bentley	**Bentley Carr**, born Kansas, c.1873 (Kansas City, Kansas, 1930 US census)
Buick	**Buick Woolfross Cooper**, born Westbourne, Sussex, 1860
Cadillac	**Cadillac Berger**, married Jeanne Cherel, Rennes, France, 21 May 1686
Caprice	**Caprice Aston**, died Weston-super-Mare, Somerset, 1942
Car Chase	**Car Chase**, born Brook, Hampshire, c.1858 (Titchfield, Hampshire, 1881 census)
Caravan	**Caravan Mayleave**, born Canada, c.1857 (Androscoggin, Maine, 1870 US census)
Chevrolet	**Chevrolet Gregory**, died Chatham, Georgia, USA, 7 September 1946
Daimler	**Donald Daimler Evans**, born Cardiff, Glamorgan, 1909
Datsun	**Datsun Crawly**, born Virginia, c.1858 (Lunenburg, Virginia, 1880 US census)
Delorean	**Delorean Carr**, died Kenton, Kentucky, USA, 17 June 1914. *The DeLorean DMC-12 sports car became famous as the time machine in the film* Back to the Future *(1985).*
Dodge	**Dodge Bentley**, born Kansas, c.1904 (Hill, Kansas, 1920 US census)
Esso	**Esso Reynolds**, born Georgia, USA, 15 December 1905; died Cleveland, Ohio, 29 January 1993

Ferrari	**Ferrari Sierra**, born Argentina, c.1895 (Buenos Aires, Argentina, 1895 Argentina census)
Focus	**Focus White**, born New Brunswick, Canada, c.1853 (Westmorland, New Brunswick, 1891 Canada census)
Ford	**Ford Carr**, born Newcastle upon Tyne, Northumberland, c.1863 (Newcastle upon Tyne, 1871 census)
Frontera	**Frontera Clay**, born 22 December 1910; died Oakland, California, USA, 1 August 1989
Garage	**Garage Hulse**, married Great Boughton, Cheshire, 1860
Gasoline	**Gasoline McKenzie Yeats**, born Manchester, Lancashire, 1845
Harley Davidson	**Harley Davidson**, born Cainham, Shropshire, c.1879 (Cainham, 1881 census)
	Harley Davidson Webster, born 30 December 1924; died Sacramento, California, USA, 6 September 1994
Hatch Back	**Henry Hatch Back**, father of Clara Lee Back, born North Carolina, USA, 26 July 1902
Honda	**Honda White**, born Limehouse, London, c.1858 (London, 1881 census)
Hummer	**Hummer Dewar**, born Jamaica, c.1816 (Barony, Lancashire, 1851 Scotland census)
Jaguar	**Jaguar Bono**, died California, USA, 24 July 2000
Jeep	**Jeep Ida**, born Iowa, c.1890 (Coleridge, Nebraska, 1920 US census)

Lada	**Lada Morgan**, born Colorado, USA, *c*.1853 (Kensington, London, 1881 census)
Lamborghini	**Vienna Lamborghini Ferranti**, born Italy, *c*.1857; passenger on *Aller*, Genoa, Italy–New York, USA, arrived 19 November 1902
Lancia	**Lancia Cooper**, born North Carolina, *c*.1907 (Alamance, North Carolina, 1920 US census)
Lexus	**Lexus Black**, born Tennessee, *c*.1859 (McNairy, Tennessee, 1860 US census)
Limousine	**Limousine Reese**, born 1 March 1917; died Chesapeake, Virginia, USA, 10 April 2002
Lotus	**Lotus Carr**, died Travis, Texas, USA, 19 May 1970
Maserati	**Maserati Mario**, born Italy, *c*.1884 (San Miguel Colorado, 1920 US census)
Mazda	**Mazda August**, born Iowa, 19 March 1921; died Santa Clara, California, USA, December 1980
Mercedes	**Mercedes Ben**, born Iowa, *c*.1899 (Dubuque, Iowa, 1910 US census)
	Mercedes Bentley, born *c*.1899 (Douglas, Arizona, 1930 US census)
	Mercedes Carr, born Tennessee, *c*.1900 (Sumner, Tennessee, 1920 US census)
	Mercedes Ford, born Houston, Texas, USA, 10 June 1930; died Houston, 7 May 1972
Metro	**Metro Metro**, born Russia, *c*.1875 (Snow Shoe, Pennsylvania, 1910 US census)

Mondeo	**Mondeo Hays**, born Iowa, *c.*1873 (Knox, Iowa, 1925 Iowa state census)
Morris	**Morris Driver**, born Whitechapel, London, 1859
Motor	**Motor Locker**, born Washington, 1900 (Sidney Village, Washington, 1900 US census)
Nice Carr	**Nice Carr**, born Tennessee, *c.*1844 (Macon, Tennessee, 1880 US census)
Nissan	**Nissan Nissan**, died Chicago, Illinois, USA, 14 September 1990
Opel	**Opel Wheeler**, born Iowa, 1898 (Otter Creek, Iowa, 1900 US census)
Park	**Park A. Carr**, born Tennessee, *c.*1901 (Claiborne, Tennessee, 1920 US census)

Parker	**Parker Carr**, baptized Horsted Keynes, Sussex, 5 November 1865
Petrol	**Petrol Piptone**, born Maryland, *c.*1875 (Baltimore, Maryland, 1880 US census)
Petroleum	**Petroleum Pool**, born Missouri, *c.*1879 (Athens, Missouri, 1880 US census)
Porsche	**Porsche Cayen**, born Quebec, 19 December 1889 (Quebec, 1901 Canada census)
Prius	**Arthur Prius Rudd**, buried Norwood Cemetery, Lambeth, London, 29 October 1864
Quattro	**Mary Quattro Murphy**, born 22 August 1914; died Smithfield, North Carolina, USA, 18 April 1992
Reliant	**Reliant Hawk**, born Tennessee, *c.*1878 (Cocke, Tennessee, 1920 US census)
Renault	**Renault Payment**, born Quebec, *c.*1889 (Quebec, 1891 Canada census)

Rhea Light	**Rhea Light**, born Ohio, 1895 (Shelby, Ohio, 1900 US census)
Riley	**Riley Car**, born Georgia, *c.*1849 (Richland, Arkansas, 1870 US census)
	Riley Carawan [*sic*], born 4 May 1906; died Chocowinity, North Carolina, USA, January 1985
Rolls	**Rolls Royse**, born Massachusetts, USA, 3 March 1883; died Shasta, California, 30 August 1968. There was also a Royce Rolls, born 15 January 1936, who died in Michigan, USA in April 1997.
Rover	**Rover Dover**, born Georgia, *c.*1878 (Glade Creek, Georgia, 1920 US census)
	Rover Rolls, born Cookham, Berkshire, 20 March 1891; died Swansea, Glamorgan, 1970
Saab	**Saab Hood**, born Mississippi, *c.*1890 (Pike Mississippi, 1920 US census)
Scooter	**Scooter Swindler**, born South Carolina, *c.*1866 (Jacks, South Carolina, 1870 US census)
Skoda	**Skoda Skinner**, born Iowa, USA, *c.*1896 (Fort Atkinson, Iowa, 1915 Iowa state census)
Texaco	**Texaco Wyckoff**, born 4 September 1940; died Orlando, Florida, USA, December 1991
Turbo	**Turbo Maisonet**, born Puerto Rico, *c.*1880 (Coto, Puerto Rico, 1930 US census)
Vauxhall	**Frederick Vauxhall Dent**, died Newport, Gwent, 1981

Branded!

You may love or hate the product, but Marmite is really not a suitable name for a baby, nor perhaps are any of the other brand names here, as the rest of these poor mites may have discovered on the day the school register was read out. Some, of course, are purely coincidental and long pre-date the birth of the brands with which they share a name, but the phenomenon continues today: Chanel was a very rare name before the British public became aware of French designer Coco Chanel (1883–1971), since when over 5,000 British girls have been given the first name Chanel. However, more than 700 sets of parents for whom spelling was perhaps not a strong point have created a generation of English Channels, together with more than 400 Chanells (in 2008 outnumbering the Chanels) and 100 Channells. Other luxury brands including Dior (more than 650 of them), Cartier and Versace, along with Lidl, L'Oreal, Babycham and Xerox, and not forgetting ingenious combinations such as Ryan Air, Branston Pickles and Lucas Saide, have all been chosen by British parents in recent years.

Adidas	**Adidas Jermaine Graham**, died Columbus, Ohio, USA, 22 July 2001
Allbran	**Allbran Ingrim**, born Alabama, 1885 (Jefferson, Alabama, 1900 US census)
Argos	**Argos Cowley**, married Chesterfield, Derbyshire 1876
Armani	**Armani Ford**, born Texas, 1877 (Montgomery, Texas, 1900 US census)
Asda	**Asda Burge**, born Highbridge, Somerset, c.1873 (Bath, Somerset, 1891 census)
Bacardi	**Bacardi Butler**, died Texas, USA, 16 June 2006

Big Mac	**Big Mac McDonogh**, died Jefferson, Kentucky, USA, 5 January 1987
Birdseye	**Birdseye Lingo**, born Ohio, c.1875 (Cincinnati, Ohio, 1880 US census)
Bovril	**Bovril Melts**, died Hull, Yorkshire, 1913
	Bovril Simpson, married West Ham, Essex, 1911
Cadbury	**Cadbury Jones**, born Kennington, London, c.1860 (Shoreditch, London, 1891 census)
Champagne	**Champagne Berry**, born 4 June 1958; died Lake Providence, Louisiana, USA, 23 August 2009. *Champagne is not technically a brand name, but it does have Protected Designation of Origin status.*
Chanel	**Chanel Sidebotham**, born Stalybridge, Cheshire, c.1870 (Dukinfield, Cheshire, 1891 census)
Courvoisier	**Courvoisier Smith**, died Toledo, Ohio, USA, 10 March 1993

Dior	**Dior Dillow**, born St Pancras, London, c.1877
Durex	**Durex Overholt**, born Alabama, c.1897 (Eaton, Colorado, 1910 US census)
Gucci	**Gucci Marqules**, born c.1905 (Kings, New York, 1920 US census)
Ikea	**Ikea Houseman**, born c.1851 (Otsego, Michigan, 1930 US census)
Ipad	**Ipad Campana**, born Texas, c.1907 (Livingston, Texas, 1920 US census)
Jack Daniels	**Jack Daniels Poindexter**, born 9 February 1931; died Marion, Oregon, USA, 3 November 1995
Lea Perrin	**Lea Perrin**, born 1893; died Holywell, Flintshire, 1974
Lidl	**Lidl Child**, born Iowa, c.1875 (Norfolk, Nebraska, 1885 Nebraska state census)
Marmite	**Marmite Courtney**, born c.1884 (Silver Creek, North Carolina, 1930 US census)
Moet	**Moet Laron**, born Gwinear, Cornwall, c.1850 (St Ives, Cornwall, 1911 census)
Nike	**Nike Brand**, born Austria, c.1891 (Newton, Texas, 1910 US census)
Nutella	**Nutella Walker**, born Arkansas, c.1878 (Gray, Arkansas, 1910 US census)
Pepsi	**Pepsi Cola Brown**, born 25 May 1908; died Bridgeport, Fairfield, Connecticut, USA, December 1987. *A near miss, Pepi Cola was born on 21 March 1888 and died in New York, USA, in April 1970.*
Prada	**Prada South**, born New York, c.1807 (Aubbeenaubbee, Indiana, 1850 US census)

Prindus	**Prindus Wylum**, born Arkansas, c.1858 (Red Rover, Texas, 1880 US census)
Pringles	**Pringles Lee**, born Illinois, c.1854 (Xenia, Illinois, 1870 US census)
Rolex	**Rolex Block**, born Spitalfields, London, c.1867 (Spitalfields, 1881 census)
	Rolex Willman, born Oregon, c.1901 (Union, Oregon, 1910 US census)
Sainsbury	**Sainsbury L. Sainsbury**, born Froyle, Hampshire, c.1832 (Beckington, Somerset, 1891 census)
Snickers	**Snickers Beaty**, born England, c.1862 (Humboldt, Iowa, USA, 1895 Iowa census)
Spangles	**Spangles Gipe**, born Pennsylvania, 1847 (Fairfield, Indiana, 1900 US census). *Spangles were popular boiled sweets particularly redolent of the 1970s and now discontinued.*
Starbuck	**Starbuck Jordan**, born Market Bosworth, Leicestershire, 1874
Teflon	**Teflon Jackson**, born Mississippi, 1879 (Leflore, Mississippi, 1900 US census)
Tesco	**Tesco Power**, born Warwickshire, c.1807 (Birmingham, Warwickshire, 1841 census)
Tiffany	**Tiffany Diamond**, born Pennsylvania, 1866 (Nicholson, Pennsylvania, 1900 US census)
Walker Crisp	**Walker Crisp**, born Norwich, Norfolk, 1844
Woolworth	**Woolworth Brooke**, born Malmesbury, Wiltshire, c.1849 (Malmesbury, 1881 census)

Pet Names

However much of an animal lover you may be, think very carefully: will your child thank you or curse you for saddling him or her with one of these names?

Adder   **Adder Attack**, born Hull, Yorkshire, c.1866 (Sculcoates, Yorkshire, 1881 census)

               Adder Knaggs, born Stockton-on-Tees, Durham, 1855

Albatross   **Albatross Grayson**, born 14 March 1905; died Stanislaus, Texas, USA, 3 February 1983

               Albatross Louisa Kingston, born Cookham, Berkshire, 1891

Armadillo   **Armadillo Newman**, born 19 April 1894; died Fulton, Georgia, USA, 10 August 1971

Ass   **Ass Holmes**, born Skipton, Yorkshire, 1866

Auk   **Auk Cockman**, born Illinois, c.1860 (Springfield, Illinois, 1910 US census)

Baboon   **Baboon Dalbert Anson**, born Scotland, c.1844 (Clewer, Berkshire, 1871 census)

Badger   **Badger Hunt**, born Paston, Northamptonshire, c.1888 (Paston, 1901 census)

Bat   **Bat Stack**, born Merthyr Tydfil, Glamorgan, 1858

Beaver	**Beaver Goodykoontz**, born California, USA, 14 October 1894; died Los Angeles, California, 2 June 1988
	Beaver Hunter, born Georgia, *c.*1894 (Grove Creek, Georgia, 1910 US census)
	Beaver Panter, died Kettering, Northamptonshire, 1849
Birdie	**Birdie Greenhouse**, born 11 August 1907; died Brooklyn, New York, USA, 12 November 1992
	Birdie Van Nest, born Illinois, *c.*1872 (Green Valley, Illinois, 1880 US census)
Bobcat	**Bobcat Bruce**, born Leslie, Fifeshire, *c.*1813 (Strathmiglo, Fifeshire, 1871 Scotland census)
Bunny	**Bunny Warren**, born 20 April 1911; died Dacorum, Hertfordshire, July 1998
Butterfly	**Butterfly McQueen**, born 8 January 1911; died New York, USA, 22 December 1995
Camel	**Camel Camel**, baptized St Peter and St Kevin, Dublin, Ireland, 9 August 1733
	Camel Dancer, born 8 April 1930; died Cincinnati, Ohio, USA, 10 October 1978
Cat	**Cat Dog**, baptized Dundee, Angus, 13 November 1679
	Cat Kitten, born Lawhitton, Cornwall, *c.*1820 (Launceston, Cornwall, 1851 census)
	Cat Mews, born *c.*1839; died Hexham, Northumberland, 1911
	Cat Suit, born Smyth, Virginia, USA, 12 July 1851

Chicken	**Chicken Barber**, born Alabama, *c.*1879 (Midway, Alabama, 1880 US census)
Chimp	**Chimp Norman**, born 1909; died Dacorum, Hertfordshire, 1999
Chinchilla	**Chinchilla Belt**, born Maryland, *c.*1852 (Anne Arundel, Maryland, 1880 US census)
Cockle	**Cockle Ayton**, born Depwade, Norfolk, 1842
Cod	**Cod Bohling**, died Whitechapel, London, 1880
Crab	**Crab Ironside**, born Bridport, Dorset, *c.*1858 (Thornton Hough, Cheshire, 1881 census)
Creature	**Creature Bonner**, baptized St Botolph Bishopsgate, London, 8 January 1643
	Creature Lugger, buried Sheviock, Cornwall, 23 May 1613
Cuckoo	**Cuckoo Hope Shipperson**, born Barnet, Middlesex, 1891
Dodo	**Dodo Woodcock**, married Atcham, Shropshire, 1903
Dolphin	**Dolphin Leach**, died Camberwell, London, 1911
Eel	**Eel Cherry**, married Aston, Warwickshire, 1875
Elephant	**Elephant Bill**, born California, *c.*1821 (Fresno, California, 1860 US census)
	Elephant Dick (male), born Nevada, *c.*1870 (Queen, Nevada, 1920 US census)
Elk	**Elk Mutter**, born Pitminster, Somerset, *c.*1856 (Corfe, Somerset, 1901 census)
Emu	**Emu Luckwill**, born Williton, Somerset, 1864

Ferret	**Ferret Furr**, born 1941; died Barnet, Hertfordshire, April 2002
Fish	**Fish Fish**, born Salford, Lancashire, 1840
Flea	**Flea Gray**, born 11 November 1899; died New York, USA, August 1979
Fly	**Fly Burt**, born Plymouth, Devon, 1897
Foxy	**Foxy Fox**, born 1947; died Bangor, Caernarvonshire, 1999
Gazelle	**Gazelle George**, married Flegg, Norfolk, 1873
Giraffe	**Giraffe House**, died Jefferson, Alabama, USA, 28 August 1917
Goat	**Goat Skippen**, died Wangford, Suffolk, 1858
Gorilla	**Gorilla Cook**, born Georgia, c.1867 (Milltown, Georgia, 1910 US census)
Grasshopper	**Grasshopper Arrowsmith**, born Kansas, c.1875 (Geneva, Nebraska, 1880 US census)
Hamster	**Hamster C. Armatys**, born Clerkenwell, London, c.1853 (Headingley, Yorkshire, 1901 census)
Herring	**Herring Sly**, born Walsall, Staffordshire, c.1845 (Walsall, 1871 census)
Hippo	**Hippo Manis**, born 18 May 1922; died San Mateo, California, USA, 26 November 1993

Hornet	**Hornet Hunk**, born West Cowes, Isle of Wight, c.1812 (Northwood, Hampshire, 1881 census)
Horse	**Horse Browe Trist**, born c.1800; died Godstone, Surrey, 1877
Kangaroo	**Kangaroo Fuller**, died Dallas, Texas, USA, 23 January 1963
Lamprey	**Lamprey Karney**, born Eastry, Kent, 1838
Larva	**Larva Beatrice Jeffries**, born Hereford, 1892
Leopard	**Leopard Prime**, born Chesterton, Cambridge, 1874
Lizard	**Lizard Booth**, born Sheffield, Yorkshire, 1838
Locust	**Locust Fosburg**, born Leatherhead, Surrey, c.1887 (Camberwell, London, 1891 census)
Magpie	**Magpie Ginger**, born c.1849; died Sedbergh, Yorkshire, 1902
Mammal	**Mammal Edwards**, died Pontypool, Monmouthshire, 1846
Mice	**Mice Smith**, born Cradley, Herefordshire, c.1867 (Suckley, Worcestershire, 1871 census)
Mole	**Mole Lory**, born Chertsey, Surrey, 1882
Monkey	**Monkey Ward**, born 10 April 1891; died Keokuk, Iowa, USA, June 1971
Mosquito	**Mosquito West**, born Kentucky, 1840 (Pontiac, Illinois, 1900 US census)
Moth	**Moth Hunt**, born Middlesex, c.1821 (Hillingdon, Middlesex, 1841 census)

Mouse	**Mouse Bishop**, born Virginia, 1885 (Lee, Virginia, 1900 US census)
Newt	**Newt Gawthrop**, married North Bierley, Yorkshire, 1901
Nightingale	**Nightingale Cuckoo**, died Westminster, London, 1838
Ostrich	**Ostrich Pockinghorn**, married St Stephens by Saltash, Cornwall, 1792
Otter	**Otter Bloodworth**, died Peterborough, Northamptonshire, 1842
	Otter Otters, died Mile End, London, 1868
Oyster	**Oyster Gamble**, born 28 April 1919; died Williamsburg, South Carolina, USA, July 1981
Panda	**Panda Smith**, born Ohio, c.1862 (Pleasant, Ohio, 1880 US census)
Peacock	**Peacock Prettyman** (male), baptized St Botolph, Aldgate, London, 18 August 1727
Pelican	**Pelican Nelson**, born New York, c.1870 (New York, 1870 US census)
Phoenix	**Phoenix Phoenix**, born Virginia, c.1813 (Wilkes Barre, Pennsylvania, 1880 US census)
Pig	**Pig Walker**, born Texas, c.1860 (Camp, Texas, 1880 US census)
Piggy	**Piggy Banks**, born Kimmeridge, Dorset, c.1810 (East Stonehouse, Devon, 1851 census)
	Piggy Hart, born Chorley, Lancashire, 1852

Pilchard	**Pilchard Macksey**, born Liverpool, Lancashire, c.1871 (Litherland, Lancashire, 1891 census)
	Pilchard Moore, born Sussex, Delaware, USA, 29 June 1886
Plaice	**Plaice Banks**, died Bedale, Yorkshire, 1906
Puffin	**Puffin Baskerville**, born Virginia, c.1909 (Mecklenburg, Virginia, 1920 US census)
Python	**Python Howsam**, born Pontesbury, Shropshire, c.1900 (Pontesbury, 1901 census)

Rabbit	**Rabbit Martin**, born Hampshire, c.1835 (Otterbourne, Hampshire, 1841 census)
Salamander	**Salamander Jones**, born Virginia, c.1871 (Philadelphia, Pennsylvania, 1920 US census)
Salmon	**Salmon Headache**, born South Dakota, c.1845 (South Rouse, South Dakota, 1910 US census)
Sealion	**Sealion White**, born California, c.1860 (Arena, California, 1910 US census)
Shrew	**Shrew Hugh**, born Missouri, 1875 (Kansas City, Missouri, 1900 US census)

Skunk	**Skunk Head**, born North Dakota, *c.*1858 (Mercer, North Dakota, 1910 US census)
Sloth	**Sloth Cleaver**, born Dunstable, Bedfordshire, 1861 (Dunstable, 1861 census)
Snake	**Snake Herring**, born Nebraska, 1899 (Vermillion City, South Dakota, 1900 US census)
Spider	**Spider G. Vonkersburg**, born 2 February 1956; died Cambridge, Massachusetts, USA, 29 March 2003
	Spider Harness, born *c.*1833 (Hancock, Illinois, 1860 US census)
Squirrell [*sic*]	**Squirrell William**, married Eliza Hitchcock, Christ Church, Brondesbury, Middlesex, 1889
Starfish	**Starfish Thompson**, born British Columbia, *c.*1905 (Owekans, British Columbia, 1911 Canada census)
Stoat	**Stoat Garlick**, born Huddersfield, Yorkshire, *c.*1881 (Almondbury, Yorkshire, 1881 census)
Stormy Petrel	**Stormy Petrel Hodgson**, born Stepney, London, 1892
Swine	**Swine King**, born Texas, *c.*1860 (Wichita Falls, Texas, 1930 US census)
Tortoise	**Tortoise Deen**, born *c.*1907 (Coffee, Georgia, 1930 US census)
Trout	**Trout Fisher**, born Baden, Germany, *c.*1787 (Clear Creek, Missouri, 1860 US census)
	Trout Kitchen, born Virginia, 1849 (Arkansas City, Kansas, 1900 US census)

Tuna	**Tuna Fish**, born Iowa, *c*.1886 (Topeka, Kansas, 1930 US census)
Turkey	**Turkey Legs**, born *c*.1865 (Oklahoma, 1895 US Indian census)
Turtle	**Turtle King**, married Sheffield, Yorkshire, 1887
Turtledove	**Turtledove Hancock**, married Daniel Warden, St Martin-in-the-Fields, London, 1795
Unicorn	**Unicorn Taylor**, born Sweden, *c*.1815 (Austin, Texas, 1850 US census)
Vermin	**Vermin Eastwood**, born Burnley, Lancashire, *c*.1841 (Blackpool, Lancashire, 1861 census)
Vole	**Vole Wilson**, born Eckington, Derbyshire, *c*.1827 (Eckington, 1851 census)
Weasel	**Weasel Ayres**, born Croydon, Surrey, *c*.1877 (Croydon, 1881 census)
Weevil	**Weevil Temple**, born North Carolina, *c*.1910 (Pasquotank, North Carolina, 1920 US census)
Wildcat	**Wildcat Duke**, born Alabama, *c*.1870 (Monroe, Alabama, 1870 US census)
Wildgoose	**Wildgoose Wildgoose**, born Bakewell, Derbyshire, *c*.1846 (Bakewell, 1851 census)
Winkle	**Winkle Baker**, died Medway, Kent, 2003
Wolf	**Wolf Bear Chalvony**, born St George in the East, London, 1910
	Wolf Fox, born Whitechapel, London, *c*.1876 (Whitechapel, 1881 census)

Wolf Guts, born North Dakota, c.1860
(Todd, South Dakota, 1920 US census)

Wolf Wolf, born St George in the East,
London, 1886

Worm   **Worm J. Martin**, born Honiton, Devon,
c.1884 (Honiton, 1891 census)

Zebra   **Zebra Leek**, died Birmingham,
Warwickshire, 1865

Food & Drink

While those who coo over a newborn baby may use such clichés as 'delicious' or 'good enough to eat', most would hesitate to name their child after something more commonly found in the larder or the fridge – but not the parents of these infants.

Absinthe **Absinthe Lindsey**, born Virginia, 1850 (Washington, DC, 1900 US census)

Apple Pie **Apple Pie**, born Virginia, c.1830 (Shelby, Tennessee, 1870 US census)

Bagel **Bagel Baker**, born Middlesex, c.1816 (Shoreditch, London, 1841 census)

Biscuit **Biscuit Adams**, born Georgia, c.1800 (Beech Creek, Arkansas, 1850 US census)

Butter **Butter Reynolds**, married Mile End, London, 1876

Candy **Candy Barr**, born South Carolina, c.1848 (Williamsburg, South Carolina, 1870 US census)

Cheese **Cheese Robinson**, born Alabama, c.1856 (Huntsville, Alabama, 1880 US census)

Cherry Tart **Cherry Tart**, born Mississippi, c.1859 (Yalobusha, Mississippi, 1860 US census)

Chocolate **Chocolate Ethel Jones**, born Cirencester, Gloucestershire, c.1894 (Cirencester, 1911 census)

Chutney **Chutney Jones**, died Limestone, Alabama, USA, 23 April 1915

Custard **Custard Custard**, born c.1876 (Tanners Creek, Virginia, 1930 US census)

Eclair	**Amastasius Eclair Eclair**, born Ellenburg, New York, USA, 26 December 1879; died Hyde Park, Vermont, 26 February 1923
Egan Bacon	**Egan Bacon**, born New York, c.1847 (Norwich, New York, 1850 US census)
Eggy	**Eggy Bacon**, born Georgia, c.1851 (Hawkinsville, Georgia, 1880 US census)
Gravy	**Gravy Cook**, born 18 December 1917; died USA, May 1961
Gum	**Gum Blum**, born Prussia, c.1828 (Mason, Kentucky, 1870 US census)
Ham	**Ham Burger**, born Michigan, c.1847 (Pittsford, Michigan, 1850 US census)
	Ham Sandwich, born c.1910 (New Orleans, Louisiana, 1910 US census)
Hungry	**Hungry Bill**, born Nevada, c.1851 (Eureka, Nevada, 1880 US census)
Jam	**Jam Curry**, married Tiverton, Devon, 1854
	Jam Lamb, born Fordyce, Banffshire, c.1869 (Fordyce, 1891 Scotland census)
Jelly	**Jelly Bush**, born Mississippi, c.1856 (Noxubee, Mississippi, 1910 US census)
Lasagna	**Lasagna Moore**, born 11 February 1968; died Fountain, North Carolina, USA, 18 July 2005
Lemonade	**Lemonade Danforth**, born Kansas, c.1879 (Burlingame, Kansas, 1880 US census)
Liver	**Liver Bacon**, born Missouri, c.1891 (St Charles, Missouri, 1910 US census)

Marmalade	**Marmalade Cherbert**, born 22 March 1944; died Coos Bay, Oregon, USA, 4 April 2004
	Marmalade Duke, born England, *c*.1815 (De Kalb, Illinois, 1880 US census)
Milk	**Milk Faust**, born Minnesota, USA, 1895 (Big Stone, Minnesota, Minnesota state census 1895)
Mineral Waters	**Mineral Waters**, born Shoeburyness, Essex, *c*.1893 (Shoeburyness, 1901 census)
Muffin	**Muffin Hill**, born Texas, *c*.1876 (Plantersville, Texas, 1880 US census)
Mustard	**Mustard Mustard**, born Virginia, *c*.1847 (Mechanicsburg, Virginia, 1870 US census)
Pastry	**Pastry Pattison**, born 1896 (Tallahatchie, Mississippi, 1900 US census)
Pepper	**Pepper Mixer**, born Dedham, Massachusetts, USA (*Massachusetts Name Changes, 1780–1892*). *He changed his named to Charles Mixer on 13 June 1810.*
Pickles	**Pickles Smith**, born Burnley, Lancashire, 1863
Pie	**Pie Crust Howard**, born Mississippi, 1889 (Newport, Mississippi, 1900 US census)
Porridge	**Porridge Salmon**, born Brackley, Northamptonshire, 1840
Pudding	**Pudding Rambo**, born Louisiana, *c*.1904 (Ringgold, Louisiana, 1910 US census)

Quiche	**Quiche Kalle**, born Greece, *c*.1900 (Stark, Ohio, 1920 US census)
Salami	**Salami Wingate**, born Alford, Lincolnshire, *c*.1842 (Alford, 1851 census)
Sandwich	**Sandwich Green**, resident of Coventry, Rhode Island, 1790 US census
Sardine	**Sardine Reeves**, born West Ham, Essex, 1872
Spam	**Spam Toodles**, born Maryland, *c*.1895 (Annapolis, Maryland, 1910 US census)
Spearmint	**Spearmint Hardy**, born Blandford, Dorset, 1906
Spicy	**Spicy Fudge**, born Georgia, *c*.1859 (Pinellas, 1935 Florida, USA, census)

Sugar	**Sugar Sweet** (male), born Canada, c.1853 (Webster, Massachusetts, 1880 US census)
Tart	**Tart Michelle**, born Hammersmith, c.1874 (Deptford, London, 1891 census)
Tequilla	**Tequilla Arnold**, born South Carolina, 1898 (Dunklin, South Carolina, 1900 US census)
Toast	**Toast Baker Sizum**, born Germany, c.1899; crew on *Leviathan*, Southampton, UK-New York, USA, arrived 26 April 1926
	Toast Deadman, born Texas, c.1882 (Lamar, Texas, 1910 US census)
Toffee	**Toffee Shaker**, born 23 July 1891; died Cleveland, Ohio, USA, May 1972
Treacle	**Treacle Ebersole**, born Texas, USA, 19 February 1902; died San Diego, California, 30 August 1993
	Treacle Tart, baptized Durham, 21 June 1746
Trifle	**Trifle Lafountain**, born Canada, c.1852 (Bakersfield, Vermont, 1870 US census)
Venison	**Venison Lukehart**, born Pennsylvania, c.1848 (West Mahoning, Pennsylvania, 1850 US census)
Watercress	**Watercress Joe**, born c.1829 (Burslem, Staffordshire, 1881 census)
White Bread	**White Bread**, born Illinois, c.1855 (Amboy, Illinois, 1880 US census)
Wine	**Wine Summers**, born Kingswinford, Staffordshire, c.1870 (Kingswinford, 1871 census)

Fruits & Nuts

Flower and plant names such as Iris and Violet were once common, while Lily/Lilly, Holly/Hollie, Daisy, Poppy, Jasmine and Rosie remain among the top 100 names in England and Wales. Similarly, we are aware of fruit names such as Cherry and Clementine, and are familiar with Peaches Geldof and Apple Paltrow-Martin – but along with these there are other fruits and plants that have rarely been used or are still up for grabs – if you must.

Apple
: **Apple Jordan**, born Milton, Kent, 1853

Bamboo
: **Bamboo Douglas**, died Dallas, Texas, USA, 23 July 1978

Banana
: **Banana Bill Shaw**, born 1919; died Lincolnshire, 2003

: **Banana Wymer**, born Tennessee, *c.*1873 (Newbern, Tennessee, 1910 US census). *Banana's name blends those of her parents, Ben and Annie.*

Blackberry
: **Blackberry Weaver**, married Elizabeth Harris, Wirt, Virginia, USA, 4 July 1861

Buttercup
: **Buttercup Bazalgette**, born Hull, Yorkshire, *c.*1888 (Wimbledon, 1901 census)

Cabbage
: **Cabbage String**, born Poland, 1866 (Windsor, Connecticut, 1900 US census)

Carrot
: **Carrot Harsnip**, born Horncastle, Lincolnshire, 1838

: **Carrot Organ**, born Texas, 1889 (Georgetown, Texas, 1900 US census)

Cranberry	**Cranberry T. Breckenridge**, born 25 November 1914; died Staunton, Virginia, USA, 31 March 1992
Forget-me-not	**Forget-me-not Geeves**, born Hertford, 1898
Fruit	**Fruit Pollock**, born Pennsylvania, c.1839 (Conewango, Pennsylvania, 1910 US census)
Gooseberry	**Gooseberry Berry**, born Texas, c.1882 (Dallas, Texas, 1920 US census)
Guava	**Guava Gore**, born Ohio, c.1902 (Pipestem, West Virginia, 1910 US census)
Lavender	**Lavender Marjoram**, born Mitford, Norfolk, 1848
Lemon	**Lemon Lemon**, married City of London, 1885
	Lemon Orange, baptized Newcastle-under-Lyme, Staffordshire, 28 July 1723
Lettuce	**Lettuce Down**, born Kensington, London, 1876
Loganberry	**Loganberry Perry**, born Illinois, c.1814 (Sharon, Illinois, 1920 US census)
Lychee	**Lychee Pilote**, born Quebec, c.1861 (Quebec, 1871 Canada census)
Magnolia	**Magnolia Laughinghouse**, born North Carolina, c.1879 (Chicoa, North Carolina, 1880 US census)
Mango	**Mango Smith**, born Scotland, c.1804 (Litchurch, Derbyshire, 1871 census)
Melons	**Melons Meakin**, married Basford, Nottinghamshire, 1897

Onion	**Onion Davis**, married Ann Smith, Bristol, Gloucestershire, 28 June 1720
Orange	**Orange Head**, born North Huish, Devon, c.1785 (Ugborough, Devon, 1861 census)
	Orange Lemon, born Kingston, Surrey, 1871
	Orange Snodgrass, born 31 March 1894; died Fremont, Nebraska, USA, June 1982
Pea	**Pea Green**, born Halifax, Yorkshire, 1856
Quince	**Quince Quinn**, born Missouri, c.1898 (Columbia, Missouri, 1920 US census)
Raspberry	**Raspberry King**, born Freebridge Lynn, Norfolk, 1853
	Raspberry Washington, born 30 November 1916; died Jackson, Mississippi, USA, 1 December 1995
Rhubarb	**Rhubarb Bean**, born 2 November 1916; died Bury St Edmunds, Suffolk, November 2002
Spearmint	**Spearmint Hardy**, born Blandford, Dorset, 1906
Strawberry	**Strawberry E. Presnell**, married St Olave, Southwark, London, 1888
Sycamore	**Sycamore Hyam**, married City of London, 1878
Tomato	**Tomato May**, born St Saviour, Southwark, London, 1889
Turnip	**Turnip Berry**, born Louisiana, c.1825 (Richland, Louisiana, 1870 US census)
Vine	**Vine Leaf**, born York, 1896
Walnut	**Walnut Fox**, born Virginia, c.1904 (Coles, Virginia, 1910 US census)

Home Sweet Home

While it may be unkind to suggest that some parents looked around the house for inspiration and called their kids after the first thing they saw, some of these names appear to confirm this suspicion.

Attic   **Attic Young**, born 8 January 1955; died Fort Myers, Florida, USA, April 1980

                 Sarah Ann Attic Attic, born Woodbridge, Suffolk, 1843

Basement   **Basement Ford**, born South Carolina, c.1817 (Bordeaux, South Carolina, 1870 US census)

Basin   **Basin Morgan**, born Varteg, Monmouthshire, c.1865 (Newport, Monmouthshire, 1871 Wales census)

Basket   **Basket George**, born Salford, Warwickshire, c.1835 (Evesham, Worcestershire, 1851 census)

Bath   **Mary Bath Walters**, born Kingsbridge, Devon, 1854

                 Wetta Bath Jennings, born Camelford, Cornwall, 1844

Bed   **Bed Bums**, born Ireland, c.1843 (Altrincham, Cheshire, 1871 census)

Bidet   **Bidet Divan**, born Ireland, c.1845 (Saranac, New York, 1860 US census)

Bin   **Bin Manet**, died Liverpool, Lancashire, 1956

Blender   **Blender Swock**, born Dickleburgh, Norfolk, c.1832 (Diss, Norfolk, 1871 census)

Bottle	**Bottle Bottleson**, born Norway, *c.*1819 (Dekorra, Wisconsin, 1870 US census)
Breadbin	**William Henry Breadbin Carlton**, born Hull, Yorkshire, *c.*1859 (Hull, 1881 census)
Brick	**Brick Brick**, born New Jersey, *c.*1845 (Pilesgrove, New Jersey, 1870 US census)
	Brick Wick, born Sweden, *c.*1885 (St Paul, Minnesota, 1930 US census)
	Brick Yard, born 22 April 1974; died Florida, USA, 22 April 2009
Cabinet	**Cabinet Currier**, born Ohio, *c.*1855 (Henrietta, Ohio, 1860 US census)
Candle	**Candle Clarke**, born Ipswich, Suffolk, *c.*1881 (Ipswich, 1901 census)
Carpet	**Carpet Magruder**, born Texas, *c.*1901 (San Jacinto, Texas, 1920 US census)
Cellar	**Cellar Bland**, born Arkansas, *c.*1878 (Franklin, Arkansas, 1880 US census)
Chair	**Chair Rider**, born New York, 1893 (Roseboom Township, New York, 1900 US census)
Chandelier	**Chandelier Curry**, born South Carolina, *c.*1853 (Horns Creek, South Carolina, 1870 US census)
Clock	**Clock Clayton**, born Greenwich, Kent, *c.*1844 (Northfleet, Kent, 1871 census)
Coal	**Coal Sommerville**, born Reading, Berkshire, *c.*1897 (Reading, 1901 census)
Commode	**Commode Grimes**, born Kentucky, *c.*1870 (Hickory Point, Illinois, 1930 US census)
Couch	**Couch Couch**, born Georgia, *c.*1879 (Gordon, Georgia, 1900 US census)

Cupboard	**Cupboard Middlebrooks**, born Georgia, c.1879 (Morgan, Georgia, 1880 US census)
Cushion	**Cushion Butt**, born Virginia, c.1892 (Madison, Virginia, 1910 US census)
Desk	**Desk Taylor**, born Madley, Shropshire, c.1874 (Hanley, Shropshire, 1901 census)
Dinette	**Dinette Perier**, born Virginia, c.1800 (Norfolk, Virginia, 1850 US census)
Dish	**Dish Carrington**, born Dukinfield, Cheshire, c.1892 (Nether Hoyland, Yorkshire, 1901 census)
Door	**Door Smith**, born Deptford, London, c.1883 (St Marylebone, London, 1901 census)
Dresser	**Dresser Bird**, born Utah, 1887 (Springville, Utah, 1900 US census)
Duvet	**Duvet Batesole**, born Ohio, c.1868 (Toledo, Ohio, 1870 US census)
Emory Board	**Emory Board**, born 14 January 1877 (Harrison, West Virginia, USA, World War I draft registration)

Encyclopedia Britannica

Encyclopedia Britannica Dewey, born New York, USA, 13 December 1814. *Encyclopedia Britannica Dewey did not like her first name so went by the name Brittany or Britannia. Her parents, Timothy and Beulah Dewey, also gave her eleven brothers and sisters strange names: Almira Melphomenia, Anna Diadama, Apeama, Armenius Philadelphus, Essephemia, Franklin Jefferson, Marcus Bonaparte, Octavia Ammonia, Philander Seabury, Pleiades Arastarcus and Victor Millenius.*

Fan Light	**Fan Light**, baptized West Wittering, Sussex, 20 February 1760
Fire	**Fire Broadhead Rollinson**, born Huddersfield, Yorkshire, 1865
Flannel	**Flannel Maddox**, born 5 January 1896; died Chicago, Illinois, USA, May 1979
Floor	**Floor Brown**, born North Carolina, c.1891 (Charlotte, North Carolina, 1910 US census)
Fountain Penn	**Fountain Penn**, born Virginia, c.1834 (Mayo, Virginia, 1870 US census)
Freezer	**Freezer Breeze**, born Great Yarmouth, Norfolk, c.1839 (Great Yarmouth, 1851 census)
Fridge	**Fridge Jester**, born Texas, USA, 25 October 1892; died Falls Church, Virginia, June 1973
Handle	**Handle Binns**, born Salford, Lancashire, c.1877 (Barton-upon-Irwell, Lancashire, 1881 England census)
Ironing	**Ironing Koon**, born Pennsylvania, c.1859 (Waynesborough, Pennsylvania, 1880 US census)
Jar	**Jar Leisure**, born Kentucky, c.1873 (Stanford, Kentucky, 1910 US census)
Kitchen	**Kitchen Clegg**, born Hunslet, Yorkshire, 1855
Lamp	**Lamp Munt**, born Sebergham, Cumberland, c.1833 (Sebergham, 1851 census)
Larder	**James Larder Longbottom**, born Louth, Lincolnshire, 1839
	Larder Lowe, born Wearhead, Durham, c.1860 (Darlington, Durham, 1891 census)

Lino	**Lino Fuck**, baptized São Pedro De Alcântara, Santa Catarina, Brazil, 24 February 1897
Loft	**Loft Robinson**, died Scarborough, Yorkshire, 1841
Log	**Log Ward**, born Haceby, Lincolnshire, c.1824 (Caistor, Lincolnshire, 1851 census)
Magazine	**Magazine Lemon**, born South Carolina, 1890 (Santee, South Carolina, 1900 US census)
Mattress	**Caroline Mattress Parry**, born Manchester, Lancashire, 1885
	Mattress Meyers, born Indiana, c.1898 (Henry, Indiana, 1910 US census)
Napkin	**Napkin Brooker**, born Sussex, c.1822 (Uckfield, Sussex, 1841 census)
Pantry	**Leonard Pantry Moon**, born Lambeth, London, 1890
	Pantry Samuel, born Pennsylvania, c.1899 (Newark, New Jersey, 1910 US census)
Paper	**Paper Regan**, born Ireland, c.1800 (Whitechapel, London, 1851 census)
Patio	**Patio Phicioli**, born c.1881; died Montana, USA, 26 June 1911
Piano	**Piano Smith**, born Georgia, c.1830 (Macon, Georgia, 1880 US census)
Pillow	**Pillow Gage**, died Bury St Edmunds, Suffolk, 1863
Pilot Light	**Pilot Light**, born 6 May 1902; died Dyersburg, Tennessee, USA, December 1980
Porch	**Porch Scowcroft**, born Bolton, Lancashire, 1861

Quilt	**Amy Quilt Boore**, born Nantwich, Cheshire, 1883
	William Quilt Hogg, born Sunderland, Durham, 1905
Roof	**Roof Pope**, died Warwick, 1865
	Roof Pope, died Hastings, Sussex, 1897
Rug	**Rug Miser**, born New Orleans, Louisiana, c.1854 (New Orleans, 1860 US census)
Saucer	**Saucer Collins**, born Alabama, 1875 (Mobile, Alabama, 1900 US census)
Scissors	**Aubrey Scissors Ryness**, born 1906; died Rushcliffe, Nottinghamshire, 1981
	Good Scissors Weasel, born Montana, 1859 (Teton, Montana, 1900 US census)
Sheet	**Sheet Peskett**, born Maidstone, Kent, 1844
Shelf	**Shelf Wood**, born Tennessee, c.1845 (Hardemann, Tennessee, 1880 US census)
Shower Rose	**Shower Rose**, born Virginia, c.1864 (Union, West Virginia, 1870 US census)
Sideboard	**Fannie Sideboard Johnson**, died New Orleans, Louisiana, USA, 19 March 1930
	Georgia Sideboard Stevens, died New Orleans, Louisiana, USA, November 1942
	Harriet Sideboard Johnson, born c.1852; died Baton Rouge, Louisiana, USA, 20 February 1926
Sink	**Sink Brim**, born 12 February 1886; died Harvey, Illinois, USA, April 1970
Sofa	**Sofa Couch**, born Tennessee, c.1864 (Waller, Tennessee, 1880 US census)
	Sofa Salmon, born Dunmow, Essex, 1859

Spatula	**Spatula Christacopoulos**, born Greece, c.1876 (Milwaukee, Wisconsin, 1920 US census)
Spoon	**Spoon Murrow**, born Sherborne, Durham, c.1851 (Monk Hesledon, Durham, 1861 census)
Stairs	**Stairs Walker**, born London, c.1846 (Pisley, Derbyshire, 1851 census)

Stove	**Stove Murray**, born Blackfriars, London, c.1876 (Southwark, London, 1901 census)
Table	**Table McKnew**, born Virginia, 1879 (Rich Valley District, Virginia, 1900 US census)
Tallboy	**Tallboy Binns**, born Ireland, c.1812 (Philadelphia, Pennsylvania, 1860 US census)

Teapot	**Teapot Brown**, born Louisiana, *c.*1878 (Tensas, Louisiana, 1880 US census)
	Teapot Waterhouse, born 1947; died Medway, Kent, 2002
Telephone	**Telephone Cardinal**, born Quebec, *c.*1890 (Quebec, 1891 Canada census)
Towel	**Towel Towel**, born Hungary, *c.*1891 (Niagara, New York, 1910 US census)
Trolley	**Trolley Thomas Houghton**, born Bourne, Lincolnshire, 1859
Utensil	**Utensil Pugh**, married Michael Ward, Randolph, North Carolina, USA, 6 October 1889
Vase	**Vase Purser**, died Midhurst, Sussex, 1876
Wal Paper	**Wal Paper**, born Greenwich, Kent, *c.*1864 (Greenwich, 1901 census)
Wardrobe	**Wardrobe Hudson**, born East Retford, Nottinghamshire, 1857
Water	**Water Board**, born Axbridge, Somerset, 1853
Whisk	**Whisk McDerna**, born England, 1848 (New York, 1900 US census)

Windows	**Windows Aldridge**, born Staines, Middlesex, *c.*1848 (Staines, 1861 census)

Designer Labels

A sub-genre of names derived from household furnishings, the contents of the wardrobe have provided naming inspiration for a number of desperate parents.

Bowler
: **Bowler Gnat**, born Illinois, c.1915 (Chicago, Illinois, 1920 US census)

Cashmere
: **Cashmere Brassiere**, born Pennsylvania, c.1874 (Westmoreland, Pennsylvania, 1920 US census)

Flares
: **Flares Moore**, born Birmingham, Warwickshire, c.1856 (Handsworth, Staffordshire, 1871 census)

Girdle
: **Girdle Headley**, born Great Ouseburn, Yorkshire, 1886

Handbag
: **Handbag Gean**, born Ireland, c.1865 (Ashland, Ohio, 1910 US census)

Knicker
: **Knicker Hedwig**, born Texas, c.1897 (San Angelo, Texas, 1930 US census)

Knickerbocker
: **Knickerbocker House**, born Indiana, c.1874 (Anderson, Indiana, 1880 US census)

Nylon
: **Nylon Green**, born Nova Scotia, Canada, c.1877 (Houston, Texas, 1920 US census). *He received the name 'Nylon' almost sixty years before Nylon was invented.*

Panti
: **Panti Downey**, born North Carolina, c.1865 (Sassafras Fork, North Carolina, 1870 US census)

Panties
: **Panties Moberg**, born Sweden, c.1870 (Chicago, Illinois, 1920 US census)

Pants	**Pants Schubert**, born Chiswick, Middlesex, c.1898 (Chiswick, 1901 census)
Panty	**Panty Brain**, born North Carolina, c.1909 (Leaksville, North Carolina, 1920 US census)
	Panty Coppola, married Rose Johnson, St Pancras, London, 1918
Sweater	**Sweater Glass**, born North Carolina, 1899 (Jefferson, North Carolina, 1900 US census)
Tophat	**Tophat Thasier**, born Canada, 1856 (Percy, Ontario, 1861 Canada census)
Trainers	**Trainers Wheatfield**, born St Luke, London, c.1850 (St Luke, 1860 census)
Trouser	**Trouser Smith**, born Canton, Texas, USA, 19 February 1877; died Tyler, Texas, 31 December 1968
Wellington	**Wellington Boot**, born Linton, Cambridgeshire, 1869
Welly	**Welly Fun**, born China, 1875 (Bergen, New Jersey, 1900 US census)
Zip/Zipper	**Zip Rambo**, born Louisiana, 1847 (Point Coupee, Louisiana, 1880 US census)
	Zipper Brotherwood, born Uckfield, Sussex, 1885

Disease & Destiny

It could be the clinical nature of childbirth that has led parents occasionally to alight upon some medical term or body part in determining the name – and perhaps the future happiness – of their newly born child.

Acne   **Acne Fountain**, born North Carolina, c.1871 (Richlands, North Carolina, 1930 US census)

Anaesthesia   **Anaesthesia Leech**, born 1902; died Hartlepool, Durham, 1903

Angina   **Angina Lay**, born Appleton, Berkshire, c.1860 (Appleton, 1861 census)

Appendix   **Appendix Lowder**, born Kentucky, c.1868 (Old Town, Greenup, Kentucky, 1880 US census)

Artery   **Artery Smith**, born Bedstone, Shropshire, c.1899 (Bishops Castle, Shropshire, 1901 census)

Aspirin   **Aspirin Olsen**, born Norway, c.1856 (Traill, Dakota Territory, 1880 US census)

Blood   **Blood Lillie Coffin**, born Illinois, c.1856 (Batavia, Illinois, 1870 US census)

Cholera   **Cholera Carr**, buried St Alfege, Greenwich, Middlesex, 26 May 1832

Circumcision   **Circumcision Sanchez**, born Spain, c.1902 (Youngstown, Ohio, 1930 US census)

Consumption   **Consumption Gavan**, died Jefferson, Kentucky, USA, 18 November 1869

Eczema   **Eczema Hugey**, born Ohio, 1878 (Nodaway, Missouri, 1900 US census)

Enema   **Enema Bottomley Wood**, died Huddersfield, Yorkshire, 1904

Gonads	**Gonads Anchondo**, born Mexico, c.1897 (El Paso, Texas, 1920 US census)
Guts	**Guts Rutherford**, born Texas, 1859 (Altus Township, Oklahoma, 1900 US census)
Hernia	**Hernia Harker**, born Bolton, Lancashire, 1887
Hysteria	**Hysteria Johnson**, born Sweden, c.1881 (Chicago, Illinois, 1910 US census)
Leper	**Leper Scarlett**, born Tuddenham, Suffolk, c.1845 (Tuddenham, 1901 census)
Malaria	**Malaria Strunk**, born Pennsylvania, c.1875 (Brecknock, Pennsylvania, 1880 US census)
Phlegm	**Phlegm Click**, born Kentucky, c.1880 (Rowan, Kentucky, 1920 US census)
Piles	**Piles Edycle Cradock**, born Somerset, c.1840 (West Derby, Lancashire, 1861 census)
Placenta	**Placenta Hightshoe**, born Ohio, c.1839 (Sylvester, Wisconsin, 1860 US census)
Plague	**Plague Hopp**, born Wisconsin, c.1885 (Westford, Wisconsin, 1910 US census)
Poxy	**Poxy Pann**, born c.1904 (Philadelphia, Pennsylvania, 1930 US census)
Puke	**Puke Kenington**, born South Carolina, c.1796 (Pike, Alabama, 1850 US census)
Sick	**Sick Catlett**, born Over, Cambridgeshire, c.1863 (Willesden, Middlesex, 1901 census)
Smallpox	**Smallpox Tommy**, born Florida, c.1887 (Lee, Florida, 1930 US census)
Sore	**Sore Ass**, born Russia, c.1897; passenger on *Russia*, Libau, Latvia–New York, USA, arrived 9 March 1914

Thrush	**Thrush Burns** (female), born Ireland, c.1845 (Boston, Massachusetts, 1880 US census)
Tonsil	**Tonsil Beard**, born Arkansas, c.1872 (Cache, Arkansas, 1930 US census)
	Tonsil Queen, born Georgia, c.1875 (Bryant, Georgia, 1910 US census)
Tonsilliti	**Tonsilliti Jackson**, born 7 November 1932; died Long Beach, California, USA, 26 May 2006
Typhus	**Typhus Black**, born Arkansas, c.1897 (Gaston, Arkansas, 1920 US census)

What Did You Call Me?

I t's not exactly going to give your child a great
start in life if you give him or her a name that
sounds like an insult...

Absurd **Absurd Wilcox**, resident of Denmark
Town, New York, USA (1860 New York
state census)

Awful **Awful Parker**, born Tennessee, *c.*1859
(Dyer, Tennessee, 1880 US census)

Bad **Bad Ass**, born *c.*1888 (South Dakota,
1891 US Indian census). *Bad Ass was the
sister of Smells Good.*

Baldy **Baldy Wiggins**, born North Carolina,
1863 (Griffins, North Carolina,
1900 US census)

Barmy **Barmy Biglake**, born Illinois, *c.*1886
(Chicago, Illinois, 1920 US census)

Barmy McSherry, born Ireland, *c.*1810
(Canandaigua, New York, 1880 US census)

Bastard **Bastard Bull**, died Plomesgate,
Suffolk, 1839

Batty **Batty Ball**, born North Meols,
Lancashire, *c.*1797 (North Meols, 1871
census)

Batty Treasure, born Midsomer Norton,
Somerset, *c.*1795 (Midsomer Norton,
1861 census)

Bent **Bent Beaumont**, born Ashton-under-Lyne,
Lancashire, 1845

Bent Hardon, born Vermont, *c.*1848
(Vermont, 1860 US census)

Berk	**Berk Hunt**, born St Pancras, London, *c.*1898 (St Pancras, 1901 census). *A name that is curiously redolent of 'Berkshire Hunt', the origin of a well-known four-letter rhyming slang word.*
Camp	**Camp Henry**, born Islington, London, *c.*1840 (Islington, 1901 census)
Cockhead	**Cockhead Helen**, born Bishopston, Wiltshire, *c.*1846 (Swindon, Wiltshire, 1861 census)
Crappy	**Crappy James**, born Pennsylvania, *c.*1862 (Rahn, Pennsylvania, 1870 US census)
Craven	**Craven Tart**, born North Carolina, USA, 22 March 1917; died North Carolina, 11 January 1992
Crazy	**Crazy Jim**, born 18 July 1933; died Milwaukee, Wisconsin, USA, 16 March 2002
Creep	**Creep Easy**, born Alabama, *c.*1887 (Jefferson, Alabama, 1910 US census)
Cruel	**Cruel John Crane**, born Shropshire, *c.*1885 (Shifnal, Shropshire, 1891 census)
Daffy	**Daffy Dingle**, born Delaware, *c.*1835 (Baltimore, Delaware, 1880 US census)
	Daffy Lagerdick, born Austria, *c.*1891 (Union, New Jersey, 1910 US census)
Daft	**Daft Coggins**, born Nottingham, 1859
Dim	**Dim McTavish**, born Argyll, *c.*1849 (Argyll, 1851 Scotland census)
Dippy	**Dippy Day**, born Texas, 1878 (San Marcos, Texas, 1900 US census)

Dirty	**Dirty King**, died Hatfield, Hertfordshire, 1863
Ditsy	**Ditsy Millard**, born Land's End, Cornwall, c.1876 (West Moors, Dorset, 1901 census)
Dork	**Dork Holmes**, born Huddersfield, Yorkshire, 1905
Dumbo	**Dumbo Willans**, born 1918; died Truro, Cornwall, 2004
Effing	**Effing Dick**, born Glasgow, Lanarkshire, c.1848 (Glasgow, 1861 Scotland census)
Evil	**Evil Dennis**, born Llanelli, Carmarthenshire, 1884
Faggy	**Faggy Jennings**, born Buckinghamshire, c.1781 (Chesham, Buckinghamshire, 1841 census)
Failure	**Failure Radley**, born Lambeth, London, 1864
Fat/Fatty	**Fat Ho**, born Hawaii, c.1865 (Honolulu, Hawaii, 1910 US census)
	Fat Kock, born Hong Kong, c.1889; crew on *Colusa*, Hong Kong–San Francisco, California, USA, arrived 18 July 1913
	Fat Meat Fields, born Mississippi, 1897 (Holmes, Mississippi, 1900 US census)
	Fatty Atkinson, born Hull, Yorkshire, c.1868 (Kingston upon Hull, Yorkshire, 1881 census)
	Fatty Begay, born 15 April 1887; died Gallup, New Mexico, USA, May 1980
	and, strangely, another – although it was not a trend that caught on:
	Fatty Begay, born 15 December 1889; died Chinle, Arizona, USA, October 1971

Fatal	**Fatal Frederick Grucutt**, born Walsall, Staffordshire, 1858
Feeble	**Feeble Sutcliffe**, born Erringden, Yorkshire, *c.*1880 (Erringden, 1881 census)
Fiend	**Fiend Boothroyd**, born Huddersfield, Yorkshire, 1850
Filthy	**Filthy Thiele**, born *c.*1879, German subject (Hampstead, London, 1901 census)
Flabby	**Flabby Hubbert**, born Georgia, *c.*1850 (Natchitoches, Louisiana, 1870 US census)
Flaky	**Flaky Polk**, born North Carolina, 1850 (Lanesboro, North Carolina, 1900 US census)
Freak	**Freak E. Cox**, born Carshalton, Surrey, *c.*1877 (Carshalton, 1891 census)
	Freak Ustick, buried Egloshayle, Cornwall, 1730
Friggin	**Friggin Lawer**, married Freebridge Lynn, Norfolk, 1838
Frightful	**Frightful Brown**, born *c.*1886 (Attercliffe, Yorkshire, 1871 census)
Furious	**Furious Andrews**, born Great Horwood, Buckinghamshire, *c.*1821 (Steeple Claydon, Buckinghamshire, 1881 census)
Gaga	**Gaga Pope**, born Mississippi, *c.*1866 (Plumb Point, Mississippi, 1880 US census)
Geek	**Geek Allen**, born Massachusetts, *c.*1898 (Somerville, Massachusetts, 1920 US census)

Ghoul	**Ghoul Hall**, born Kentucky, c.1891 (Saline, Ohio, 1930 US census). *His son (born c.1925) bore the same name.*
Goon	**Goon Eccles**, born Pimlico, London, c.1841 (Chelsea, 1891 census)
Grouchy	**Grouchy Gangloff**, born 20 August 1902; died Gonzales, Louisiana, USA, January 1973
Grudgeworthy	**Grudgeworthy Grudgeworthy**, baptized Winkleigh, Devon, 21 February 1736
Harlot	**Harlot Duncan**, married Glanford Brigg, Lincolnshire, 1867
	Harlot Price (male), born Shropshire, c.1832 (Clun, Shropshire, 1841 census)
Hopeless	**Hopeless Evans**, born Stoke-on-Trent, Staffordshire, 1880
Horrible	**Horrible Richel**, born Canada, c.1910 (North Attleborough, Massachusetts, 1930 US census)
Horrid	**Horrid Griffin**, born Mississippi, c.1878 (Adams, Mississippi, 1880 US census)
Idiot	**Idiot Lony**, born Alabama, c.1852 (Elmore, Alabama, 1870 US census)
Imbecile	**Imbecile Crazy**, born c.1846 (Utah, 1887 US Indian census)
Libertine	**Libertine Moss**, married Ashton-under-Lyne, Lancashire, 1855
Loon/Loonie	**Loon Alexander Edgar**, born Eastry, Kent, 1893
	Loonie Fattelay, married Lewisham, London, 1908
Loser	**Loser Snodgrass**, born Ohio, c.1861 (Stokes, Ohio, 1880 US census)

Lousy	**Lousy Butler**, born Bradford, Yorkshire, 1885
Mad	**Mad Fontheim**, married Hampstead, London, 1903

Mad Hatter, born Wigginton, Oxfordshire, c.1879 (Northfield, Worcestershire, 1901 census). *Coincidentally, Oxfordshire was the location of Lewis Carroll's Alice in Wonderland.*

Mad Looney, born 7 March 1910; died Warwickshire, 1894

Mad Parrott, born Piedmont, Italy, c.1821 (St George Hanover Square, London, 1861 census)

Mad Price, born Bishop Auckland, Durham, c.1865 (Bishop Auckland, 1891 census)

Madman	**Madman Lumpkin**, born South Carolina, c.1898 (Lykesland, South Carolina, 1920 US census)
Maniac	**Maniac Keene**, born Chertsey, Surrey, c.1860 (Chertsey, 1861 census)
Mental	**Mental Harris**, born Russia, c.1885 (Leeds, Yorkshire, 1891 census)
Miserable	**Miserable Lorenz**, born Italy, c.1885 (Woodbury, New York, 1910 US census)
Misery	**Misery Constant**, born North Carolina, c.1898 (White Oak, North Carolina, 1910 US census)
Molester	**Molester Musky Davis**, born Johnson, North Carolina, USA, 7 November 1884; died Wilson, North Carolina, 17 November 1943
Monster	**Monster Cherry**, born Florida, c.1904 (Bland, Florida, 1910 US census)
Moron	**John Moron Battey**, born Plumboro, Derbyshire, c.1879 (Cudworth, Yorkshire, 1901 census)
	Moron Crossley, died Lunesdale, Lancashire, 1896
Morose	**Morose Phillips**, born Fenton, Staffordshire, c.1886 (Burslem, Staffordshire, 1891 census)
Muck	**Muck Bang**, born China, 1853 (Liberty and Union Townships, California, 1900 US census)
	J. Muck Fuqua, died Andalusia, Alabama, 26 April 1934
Mucky	**Mucky Haddock**, born North Carolina, c.1894 (Swift Creek, North Carolina, 1920 US census)

Muppet	**Muppet Adams**, born Arkansas, c.1904 (Newport, Arkansas, 1930 US census)
Narky	**Narky Brewer**, born Alabama, c.1890 (Jefferson, Alabama, 1920 US census)
Nasty	**Nasty Clough**, born Yorkshire, c.1786 (Bowdon, Cheshire, 1861 census)
	Nasty Elizabeth Halsey, born Berkhamsted, Hertfordshire, 1882
Nerdy	**Nerdy Spring**, born Louisiana, c.1907 (Winn, Louisiana, 1910 US census)
Notorious	**Notorious Mosley**, died Chicago, Illinois, USA, 31 December 1986
Nutty	**Nutty Bullock**, born North Carolina, c.1858 (Townsville, North Carolina, 1880 US census). *She was named after her grandmother, another Nutty Bullock.*
	Nutty Haddock, died Plomesgate, Suffolk, 1859
	Nutty Slack, born Italy, c.1864 (Islington, London, 1881 census)
Obese	**Obese Burke**, born Louisiana, c.1902 (Lafourche, Louisiana, 1920 US census)
Odd	**Odd Albert**, born 2 September 1894; died Belmar, New Jersey, USA, April 1983
Odious	**Odious Nutt**, born 17 June 1879; died Navarro, Texas, USA, 3 September 1965
Ogre	**Ogre Bee**, born Ireland, c.1883 (Manhattan, New York, 1910 US census)
Perverte	**Perverte Swanger**, born Germany, c.1841 (Galveston, Texas, 1850 US census)
Perverto	**Perverto Garza**, born Texas, c.1872 (Caldwell, Texas, 1910 US census)

Ponce	**Ponce Smith**, born Hellington, Shropshire, c.1833 (Chorlton-cum-Hardy, Lancashire, 1891 census)
Porker	**Porker Tucker**, born c.1849 (Stoke, Somerset, 1871 census)
Prickhead	**Prickhead Whelan**, born St Helens, Lancashire, c.1858 (Widnes, Lancashire, 1861 census)
Psycho	**Kathleen Psycho Houghton**, born Oxford, 1878
Putrid	**Putrid Ida Kirk**, born Tennessee, c.1835 (Maury, Tennessee, 1930 US census)
	Putrid Quasigreek N. Hebran, born Manchester, Lancashire, c.1851 (Manchester, 1881 census)
Queer	**Queer Selina Victoria Hert**, born Hamworthy, Dorset, c.1879 (Branksome, Dorset, 1901 census)
Raving	**Raving Washington**, born Georgia, c.1878 (Burke, Georgia, 1880 US census)
Reckless	**Reckless Baker**, born North Carolina, c.1846 (Ingrams, North Carolina, 1870 US census)
Rough	**Rough And Ready Shoots**, born Wisconsin, c.1848 (Moreau, Missouri, 1860 US census)
Rude	**Rude Nolan**, married Gravesend, Kent, 1857
Sadist	**Sadist Thomas**, born Texas, c.1867 (Limestone, Texas, 1880 US census)
Scary	**Scary Butts**, born Kentucky, c.1888 (Simpson, Kentucky, 1910 US census)
	Scary Looker, born Warrington, Lancashire, c.1841 (Warrington, 1851 census)

Seedy	**Seedy Mary Cooper**, born Llanelly, Monmouthshire, 1901
Sicko	**Sicko Beer**, born Holland, *c.*1869 (Leeds, Minnesota, 1910 US census)
Simple	**Simple Simon**, born Poland, *c.*1865 (Nashville, Tennessee, 1930 US census)
Slag	**Slag Johnson**, born Iceland, *c.*1853 (Selkirk, Manitoba, 1891 Canada census)
Slapper	**Slapper Clarke**, born Virginia, 1874 (Essex, New Jersey, 1900 US census)
Slimy	**Slimy Brown**, born New York, *c.*1830 (Lower Chanceford, Pennsylvania, 1860 US census)
Slutty	**Slutty Bird** (female), born Oklahoma, *c.*1909 (Eufaaula, Oklahoma, 1910 US census)
Snooty	**Snooty Scott**, born Tennessee, 1892 (Rutherford, Tennessee, 1900 US census)
Soppy	**Soppy Leggs**, born Bethnal Green, London, *c.*1841 (Bethnal Green, 1901 census)
Spoilt	**Spoilt Eliza Hobbs**, born Huntingdon, 1871
Spotty	**Spotty Bell**, married Henrietta Cooper, Lowndes, Mississippi, USA, 19 May 1883
Stinky	**Stinky Burhouse**, born Holland, *c.*1823 (Spring Lake, Michigan, 1870 US census)
Strange	**Strange Milliner**, married Emma Moore, Faversham, Kent, 1859
	Strange Young Mann, born Mechanicsburg, Ohio, *c.*1822 (Goshen, Ohio, 1850 US census); married Union, Ohio, 13 December 1866

Thick	**Thick Burke**, born Ireland, *c.*1791 (Manchester, Lancashire, 1841 census)
Touchy	**Touchy Brown**, born Tennessee, *c.*1875 (Williamson, Tennessee, 1880 US census)
Ugly	**Ugly Plug**, born Washington, *c.*1810 (Lewis, Washington, 1880 US census)
Vandal	**Vandal Mason**, born Wirral, Cheshire, 1895
Vile	**Vile Ditto**, born 5 May 1910; died Lima, Ohio, USA, 12 January 1960
Wacko	**Wacko Snead**, born North Carolina, *c.*1853 (Henderson, North Carolina, 1880 US census)
Wanton	**Wanton Coward**, born Warminster, Wiltshire, *c.*1863 (Warminster, 1871 census)
Weird	**Weird Boomgaarden**, born 12 December 1889; died South Dakota, USA, January 1965
Whalebelly	**Whalebelly Robert**, born Saham Toney, Norfolk, *c.*1818 (Saham Toney, 1861 census)

The Fame Game

Film stars, cartoon characters, TV performers, sportspeople, singers, heroes and villains have long influenced the name choices of parents – there have been over 2,000 Britneys in the UK alone since Britney Spears appeared on the scene in the late 1990s, and since 2001 more than 250 girls have been given the name Beyoncé, while such names as Albert Einstein, Lex Luther and Metallica have all been bestowed in recent years. This pattern has a long history and, of course, unless the parents of Beatles Dowler and Indiana Jones had particularly effective crystal balls, many of the names here are purely coincidental (there were more than 400 Harry Potters in England and Wales in the nineteenth century, as well as twenty boys with the first names 'Harry Potter'), while in certain instances it was almost inevitable: if your surname is Kipling, it would be hard to resist the temptation to call your son Rudyard – after all, everyone else will. One hidden danger in this route is that the famous person in question may fall out of favour – you don't often meet a little Adolf these days, but even naming your baby after a tyrannical figure did not deter some parents.

Abba	**Abba Funk**, born St George in the East, London, 1900
Adolf/Adolph	**Adolf Hitt**, born Germany, c.1871 (Willesden, London, 1901 census)
	Adolph Fuhrer, born Germany, c.1868 (Ystradyfodwg, Glamorgan, 1901 Wales census). *Fuhrer's son Leo Adolph Fuhrer was born in Pontypridd, Glamorgan, in 1898, but died in infancy, thus avoiding problems he might have encountered with his name in his forties.*

Agatha Christie	**Agatha Christie Stevenson**, born 19 March 1927; died Volusia, Florida, USA, 11 April 1985
Archimedes	**Archimedes Muff**, born Hunsworth, Yorkshire, *c.*1819 (Hunsworth, 1861 census)
Atilla [*sic*]/Attila	**Atilla Hunsicke**, born Pennsylvania, 1853 (Heidelberg, Pennsylvania, 1900 US census)
	Attila Huntington, born New York, 1852 (Somerset, New York, 1900 US census)
Beatles	**Beatles Dowler**, born Missouri, *c.*1872 (Crawford, Missouri, 1880 US census)
Benito Mussolini	**Benito Mussolini Buckross**, born 1932; died Bradford, Yorkshire, 1997. *What may have sounded like an interesting choice of first name when the fascist dictator was allegedly making the Italian trains run on time perhaps seemed less appealing ten years later.*
Beyonce	**Beyonce Gill**, born *c.*1887; passenger on *Ballarat*, Sydney, Australia–London, UK, arrived 25 August 1924
Boadicea	**Boadicea Basher**, baptized St Hilary, Cornwall, 13 January 1856
Bonaparte	**Bonaparte Smallbone**, born Guildford, Surrey, 1861
Boney M	**Boney M. Case**, born North Carolina, 1892 (Crab Creek, North Carolina, 1900 US census)

Caesar	**Caesar Bowlegs**, born Oklahoma, c.1840 (Brown, Oklahoma, 1910 US census)
	Julius Caesar K. Borgia, born St Andrews, Middlesex, c.1867 (Holborn, London, 1871 census)
Caractacus	**Caractacus L. Habakkuk**, born c.1857 (Peterstone Super Montern, Glamorgan, 1881 Wales census)
Cardinal Woolsey	**Cardinal Woolsey**, born Croydon, Surrey, 1844
Charlton Heston	**Charlton Heston Bates**, died Sunderland, Durham, 2005
Cicero	**Cicero Booboo**, born Alabama, c.1854 (Limestone, Alabama, 1870 US census)
Cleopatra	**Cleopatra Needham**, born Tennessee, c.1879 (Union, Tennessee, 1910 US census). *Cleopatra was a relatively common name, but this example is coincidentally similar to 'Cleopatra's Needle', the nickname of the obelisks erected in New York in 1877 and London the following year.*
Confucius	**Confucius Tarry**, born Leicester, 1872
Copernicus	**Copernicus Mephibosheth Lynam**, born Basford, Nottinghamshire, 1898
Demosthenes	**Demosthenes Cuppa**, married City of London, 1886
Donald Duck	**Donald Duck**, born Edmonton, Middlesex, 1899. *Donald Duck was the brother of Rhoda Duck.*

El Cid	**El Cid** (female), baptized St Paul, Norwich, Norfolk, 25 April 1686
Fidel Castro	**Fidel Castro Rodriguez**, born Mexico, 9 July 1953; died Stanislaus, California, 30 October 1985
Flash Gordon	**Flash Gordon**, born 27 September 1947; died New Orleans, Louisiana, USA, 13 September 2001. *The* Flash Gordon *cartoon strip was first published on 7 January 1934.*
General Washington	**General Washington**, born Halifax, Yorkshire, 1842
George Washington	**George Washington Milkman**, married Chorlton, Lancashire, 1888
Geronimo	**Geronimo Bow**, married Cathe [*sic*] Williams, St George in the East, London, 1810
Heinrich Himmler	**Heinrich Himmler**, born 1942; died Durham, 1990
Herman Goering	**Herman Goering**, born Birmingham, Warwickshire, 1882
	Peter Herman Goering, born Birmingham, Warwickshire, 18 May 1915. *The son of the above, during World War II Goering junior changed his name to Peter Howard Girling; he died in Towcester, Northamptonshire, in 1991.*
Hitler	**Hitler Hindi Mongon**, born 1937; died Stockton-on-Tees, Durham, 2002
Hobbit	**Hobbit Hack**, born Kentucky, c.1896 (Driskill, Kentucky, 1910 US census)

Idi Amin	**Idi Amin Stanley**, died Detroit, Michigan, USA, 13 June 1996
Imhotep	**Imhotep Kedar**, born 2 July 1980; died Raleigh, North Carolina, USA, 15 January 2004
Indiana Jones	**Indiana Jones**, born Indiana, c.1815 (Van Buren, Indiana, 1850 US census)
Jedward	**Jedward Looney**, born 10 September 1896; died Linn, Oregon, USA, April 1982

Jesus	**Jesus Christ**, born 1940; died Rotherham, Yorkshire, 2004
	Jesus Smith, born Angus, c.1823 (Brechin, Angus, 1841 Scotland census)
Judas Iscariot	**Judas Iscariot Burton**, born Stafford, 1882
Julius Caesar	**Julius Caesar**, married Alice Dente, Mitcham, Surrey, 10 April 1596
King Cole	**King Cole**, born Wortley, Yorkshire, 1883
King George	**King George**, baptized St Martin-in-the-Fields, London, 27 May 1724
King Lear	**King Lear**, born Kington Magna, Dorset, c.1898 (Kington Magna, 1901 census)
King Solomon	**King Solomon Coe**, born Caxton, Cambridgeshire, 1893
Lady Godiva	**Lady Godiva A. Wright**, born Brixton, Devon, c.1849 (Plymouth, Devon, 1891 census)
Lenin	**Lenin Smith**, born 22 January 1924; died Hampstead, New Hampshire, USA, January 1986
Marie Antoinette	**Marie Antoinette L. Robust**, married St Marylebone, London, 1905
Micky Mouse	**Micky Mouse**, married Dorothy Collett, Totternhoe, Bedfordshire, 13 May 1641
Mona Lisa	**Mona Lisa Clelland**, born Ohio, c.1903 (San Francisco, California, 1920 US census)

Monte Cristo	**Monte Cristo T. Barton**, born Lambeth, London, 1898
Nanki Poo	**Nanki Poo Sutton**, born Bristol, Gloucestershire, *c.*1887 (Bristol, 1891 census). *His parents had no doubt seen the recent debut of Gilbert and Sullivan's* The Mikado.
Napoleon	**Napoleon Bona**, born New York, *c.*1859 (Chazy, New York, 1870 US census)
	Napoleon Waterloo, born Illinois, USA, *c.*1913; died Chicago, Illinois, 11 May 1957
Pontius Pilate	**Pontius Pilate Hughes**, born Dewsbury, Yorkshire, 1872
Popeye	**Popeye Womack**, died Caswell, North Carolina, 11 January 1939
Princess Diana	**Princess Diana Shay**, born 16 June 1968; died Lambeth, London, December 2005

Robinson Crusoe	**Robinson Crusoe**, born Devon, c.1811 (Stoke Damerel, Devon, 1841 census)
Rudyard Kipling	**Rudyard Kipling Reed**, born 1929; died Poole, Dorset, 1989
Rupert Bear	**Rupert Bear**, born Stratford, Essex, c.1878 (Harrow, Middlesex, 1881 census)
Sergeant Pepper	**Sergeant Pepper**, born 12 May 1907; died Gladwyne, Pennsylvania, USA, March 1982
Socrates	**Socrates Demosthenes Westmoreland**, born Knaresborough, Yorkshire, 1853
Stalin	**Joseph Stalin Tipple**, born 1942; died Dewsbury, Yorkshire, 1999
Sweeny Todd	**Sweeny Todd**, born Marylebone, London, c.1845 (St George in the East, London, 1881 census). *Since he described himself as a barber* (Sweeney Todd, the Barber of Fleet Street *had premiered in London in 1865) and other inhabitants in his lodging house included Dick Turpin and Dutch-born Thomas Treacle, this may be an example of a census spoof.*
Tarzan	**Tarzan Mallory** (female), born South Carolina, c.1837 (Fairview, South Carolina, 1880 US census)
Tintin	**Tintin Liner**, born Georgia, c.1869 (Tallapoosa, Georgia, 1880 US census)
Virginia Woolf	**Virginia Woolf McCoy**, born 17 October 1898; died Broward, Florida, USA, 25 February 1989

Potty Names

As nappies and years of toilet-training beckon, the thoughts of a number of parents appear to have turned to bodily functions in choosing their baby's name.

Crap   **Crap Angle**, born North Carolina, *c.*1853 (Eagle Mills, North Carolina, 1880 US census)

                   Crap McDonald, born Tennessee, *c.*1870 (Rhea, Tennessee, 1870 US census)

Crapper   **Crapper Bird**, born Bury, Lancashire, 1870

Diarrhora   **Diarrhora Austin**, born Crawford, Iowa, USA, *c.*1881 (Denison, Iowa, 1895 Iowa state census)

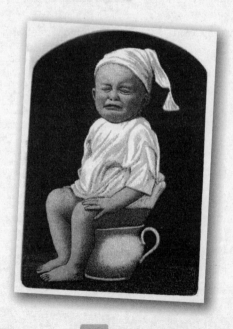

Fart	**Fart Bull**, born *c.*1851 (Montana, 1885 US Indian census)
	Fart Duck, born *c.*1881 (Colorado River, Arizona Territory, 1889 US Indian census)
	Fart Eagle, born *c.*1849 (South Dakota, 1893 US Indian census)
Farter	**Farter Craven**, born Thornton, Yorkshire, *c.*1833 (Bradford, Yorkshire, 1871 census)
Fartina	**Fartina Henwood**, born Rodbaston, Cheshire, *c.*1796 (Cheadle, Cheshire, 1851 census)
Farting	**Farting Clack**, born London, *c.*1863 (Walthamstow, Essex, 1871 census)
Farty	**Farty Archibald**, born USA, 15 November 1876 (New Westminster, British Columbia, 1901 Canada census)
	Farty Gladwish, born Hastings, Sussex, *c.*1882 (Hastings, 1901 census)
	Farty Ray, born Tennessee, *c.*1813 (Clarksville, Texas, 1860 US census)
Flushing	**Flushing Meadows**, born Shoreditch, London, 1878
Latrine	**Latrine Dubois**, born Lewisham, London, *c.*1890 (Lewisham, 1891 census)
	Latrine Topping, born Warrington, Lancashire, *c.*1871 (Warrington, 1881 census)
Loo/Lou	**Loo Loo**, born *c.*1877; died Greenwich, London, 1904
	Lou Paper, born Watford, Hertfordshire, *c.*1858 (Lambeth, London, 1891 census)
	Lou Roll, born Uxbridge, Middlesex, 1902
Pee	**Pee Taskes**, born Penzance, Cornwall, 1852

Piss	**Piss Fisher Parkinson**, born Ireland, c.1781 (Holborn, London, 1841 census)
	Piss Range, born Pennsylvania, c.1866 (La Boeuf, Pennsylvania, 1870 US census)
Pisser	**Pisser Bird**, born Georgia, c.1905 (Richmond, Georgia, 1910 US census)
Pisson	**Pisson Tubbs**, born c.1896 (Bolivar, Mississippi, 1902 US census)
Pissy	**Pissy Jordon**, born Manchester, Lancashire, c.1894 (Manchester, 1901 census)
Poo(h)	**Poo Out**, died Stepney, London, 1888
	Pooh Magraw, born Pennsylvania, c.1864 (Emlenton, Pennsylvania, 1880 US census)
Shat	**Shat Butler**, born Worcestershire, c.1834 (Oswaldslow, Worcestershire, 1841 census)
Shit	**Shit Paul**, born c.1811 (St Marylebone, London, 1841 census)
Shitton	**Shitton Brown**, born South Carolina, c.1820 (Lauderdale, Mississippi, 1850 US census)
Shitwell	**Shitwell Rogers**, born Cowick, Yorkshire, c.1827 (Ackworth,

Yorkshire, 1881 census)

Shitty	**Shitty Bunn**, born North Carolina, *c.*1869 (Springfield, North Carolina, 1870 US census)
	Shitty Dikins, born Buckinghamshire, *c.*1828 (Swanborne, Buckinghamshire, 1841 census)
	Shitty Strange, born Haselbury, Dorset, *c.*1844 (Haselbury, 1851 census)
Toilet	**Toilet Halkyard**, born Oldham, Lancashire, *c.*1839 (Northowram, Yorkshire, 1871 census)
Turd(y)	**Turd Collar**, born Ireland, *c.*1821 (St George Hanover Square, London, 1841 census)
	Turdy Brown, born Iowa, 1879 (Blaine, Butte, South Dakota, 1900 US census)
Urina	**Urina Buckett**, born Isle of Wight, 1867
Urinal	**Urinal James**, born Llanllwni, Carmarthenshire, *c.*1889 (Llanllwni, 1891 Wales census)
	Urinal Welburn, born Garton, Yorkshire, *c.*1817 (Great Driffield, Yorkshire, 1881 census)
Urine	**Urine Adkins**, born 15 June 1896; died Coeburn, Virginia, USA, March, 1972
	Urine Fartabella, born Italy, *c.*1896 (East Youngstown, Ohio, 1920 US census)
Widdle	**Widdle Chandler**, born North Carolina, *c.*1872 (Middle Fork, North Carolina, 1910 US census)

Hardly a Suitable Name for an Adult

With little thought for the possibility that their newborns might grow up to follow important professions, the parents of these children decided to give them ineffably cute names. I mean, would you wish to be treated by a doctor called Frou-Frou or be represented in court by a barrister called Tiddles?

Baby
: **Baby Bunting**, born Matlock, Derbyshire, *c*.1900 (Matlock, 1901 census)

: **Baby Weasel Fat**, born Alberta, *c*.1882 (Alberta, 1916 census of Manitoba, Saskatchewan and Alberta, Canada)

Bambam
: **Bambam House**, born Ohio, *c*.1882 (Wabash, Indiana, 1920 US census)

Bubble(s)
: **Bubble Dick**, born Kentucky, *c*.1905 (Fair, Kentucky, 1920 US census)

: **Bubbles Swadling**, born 24 July 1919; died Worthing, West Sussex, October 1996

Coyness
: **Coyness Wiggins**, born 9 December 1926; died Alabama, USA, July 1962

Cuddles
: **Cuddles Lynn**, born 1 September 1936; died Glendale, California, USA, 6 March 2004

Cute
: **Cute Hubbard**, born St Marylebone, London, *c*.1860 (St Marylebone, 1861 census)

Darling
: **Darling Dear**, born South Carolina, *c*.1807 (Newtown, Mississippi, 1860 US census)

: **Darling Donger**, born Muston, Leicestershire, *c*.1899 (Muston, 1901 census)

Delightful	**Delightful Knapp**, died Waupaca, Wisconsin, USA, 25 March 1901
Dewdrop	**Dewdrop Malone**, born 27 November 1914; died Red Bay, Alabama, USA, 15 January 2001
Diddy	**Diddy Daddilums**, born Hertfordshire, c.1874 (St Albans, Hertfordshire, 1881 census)
Dipsy	**Dipsy Campbell**, born Georgia, c.1862 (Bibb, Georgia, 1870 US census)
Fluffy	**Fluffy Heaver**, born 1901; died Kensington and Chelsea, London, 1998
Frou-Frou	**Frou-Frou Mallett**, born c.1904; died St Pancras, London, 1907
	Frou-Frou Tilley, born Bristol, Gloucestershire, c.1874 (Clifton, Gloucestershire, 1881 census)
Furry	**Furry Jane Burbidge**, born Friskney, Lincolnshire, c.1847 (Friskney, 1871 census)
	Furry Youngman, born 4 August 1896; died Ravenna, Ohio, USA, October 1979
Googoo	**Googoo Googoo**, born Nova Scotia, 25 February 1898 (Inverness, Nova Scotia, 1901 Canada census)
Honey	**Honey Moon**, born Wisconsin, c.1903 (Campbell, California, 1910 US census)
Junior	**Junior Junior**, born Alabama, c.1881 (Jefferson, Alabama, 1920 US census)
Laalaa	**Laalaa Luama**, born Finland, c.1882 (Wilkeson, Washington, 1910 US census)
Lala	**Lala Love**, died Montgomery, Alabama, January 1934

Lallu	**Lallu Lala Lad**, born 1905; died Brent, Middlesex, December 1985
Little	**Little Cox**, born Kentucky, c.1861 (Mannsville, Kentucky, 1870 US census)
	Little Dick, born Northroad, Cheshire, c.1851 (Wolstanton, Staffordshire, 1881 census)
Love	**Love Beaver** (male), born North Carolina, c.1903 (China Grove, Rowan, North Carolina, 1920 US census)
	Love Cock (female), daughter of Gabriel Cock, baptized St Columb Major, Cornwall, 3 June 1659
	Love Crapping, married Edward Addicot, Brixham, Devon, 17 February 1712
	Love Hiscock, baptized Mere, Wiltshire, 18 April 1825
	Love Morehead, born North Carolina, c.1910 (Guilford, North Carolina, 1930 US census)
	Love Reading, baptized Rickmansworth, Hertfordshire, 20 November 1768
Lovely	**Lovely Boy**, born 20 November 1915; died Rutledge, Tennessee, USA, 12 September 1992
	Lovely Cock (female), born Cornwall, c.1781 (Mylor, Cornwall, 1841 census)
	Lovely Day, born Georgia, 1892 (Round Mountain, Alabama, 1900 US census)
Lovey	**Lovey Dove**, born Georgia, c.1908 (Franklin, Georgia, 1910 US census)
Lucious	**Lucious Bacon**, born 2 August 1906; died Savannah, Georgia, USA, September 1977

Luscious	**Luscious Lemons**, born 24 July 1903; died Chickasha, Oklahoma, USA, July 1969
Moppet	**Moppet Little**, born Ireby, Cumberland, c.1857 (Crosscanonby, Cumberland, 1871 census)
Popsie	**Popsie Bottom** (female), born Kent, c.1891 (Kensington, London, 1891 census)
Precious	**Precious Green**, born Ecclesall Bierlow, Yorkshire, 1895

Rainbow	**Rainbow Sunshine**, born 5 March 1892; died New York, USA, April 1979
Snowflake	**Snowflake George Pledger**, born Hampstead, London, 1877
	Snowflake Rivett, born London, 1881
Sunny	**Sunny Day**, born Maryland, *c*.1865 (Westover, Maryland, 1910 US census)
Sweet(y)	**Sweet Hart**, died St Mary Newington, London, 1837
	Sweety Bush, born 10 September 1906; died Seattle, Washington, USA, July 1985
Sweetheart	**Sweetheart Barnes**, born *c*.1801; died Lincoln, 1881
	Sweetheart Pringle, born 25 December 1906; died Columbia, South Carolina, USA, February 1982
Tiddles	**Tiddles James**, born Kensington, London, *c*.1874 (Kensington, 1901 census)
Tinie/Tiny	**Tinie Cock**, born Pembroke, 1861
	Tiny Bird, born Texas, *c*.1876 (Melrose, Texas, 1880 US census)
	Tiny Bugg, born Georgia, 1835 (Askew, Georgia, 1900 US census)
	Tiny Hooker, born 31 March 1928; died Hartford, Connecticut, USA, May 1981
	Tiny Man, born Germany, 1839 (Tonawanda, New York, 1900 US census)
	Tiny Person, born North Carolina, *c*.1909 (Hayesville, North Carolina, 1910 US census)
	Tiny Slurd, born Plymouth, Devon, *c*.1878 (Everton, Lancashire, 1881 census)

Tinky	**Tinky Barber**, born Georgia, *c.*1876 (Dougherty, Georgia, 1880 US census)
Truelove	**Truelove Sparks**, born Kentucky, *c.*1831 (Morgan, Missouri, 1880 US census)
Twinkle	**Twinkle Slaughter**, born 3 January 1891; died Fullerton, California, USA, January 1981
Wee Girlie	**Wee Girlie Potter**, born Risbridge, Suffolk, 1906
Weeny	**Weeny Bischoff**, born *c.*1792; died Charleston, South Carolina, USA, 25 March 1862
Wieni	**Wieni Persons**, born Georgia, *c.*1889 (Talbotton, Georgia, 1900 US census)
Winsome	**Winsome Bull**, born Lambeth, London, 1896
Welcome	**Welcome Baby Darling**, born 17 October 1885; died Miami, Florida, USA, 9 December 1970
Winky	**Winky Johnson**, born Alabama, *c.*1868 (Uniontown, Alabama, 1880 US census)
Womble	**Womble Scoggins**, born *c.*1900 (Mine Creek, Arkansas, 1930 US census)
Wonderful	**Wonderful George Forsdyke**, born Bosmere, Suffolk, 1886
	Wonderful Ramsbottom, born Dewsbury, Yorkshire, 1855
	Wonderful Smith, born Blything, Suffolk, 1893
Young	**Young Love**, born Donegal, Ireland, 29 March 1788; died Pike, Ohio, USA, 20 May 1845

Snap, Crackle & Pop

Onomatopoeic first names are occasionally encountered, but are seldom advised – well, how keen would you be to spend your life introducing yourself as Smooch or Sniffle? Reading these examples out loud is rather like being present at the birth of speech...

Bash	**Bash Sharpe**, born St Coyth, Essex, c.1866 (Sculcoates, Yorkshire, 1901 England census)
Beep	**Beep McCole**, born Wisconsin, 1900 (Appleton City, Wisconsin, 1900 US census)
Belch	**Belch Clay Grasse**, born Wisconsin, c.1904 (Sheboygan, Wisconsin, 1920 US census)
Biff	**Biff Crottey** (female), born Birmingham, Warwickshire, c.1818 (Coventry, Warwickshire, 1881 census)
Boing	**Boing Wright**, born Florida, c.1892 (Alachua, Florida, 1920 US census)
Bong	**Bong Park**, born 14 May 1886; died Honolulu, Hawaii, USA, July 1969
Bubble	**Bubble Gay**, born 17 October 1927; died Humphrey, Arkansas, USA, 10 February 1992
Buzz	**Buzz Hoover**, born 30 January 1891; died Pampa, Texas, USA, October 1974
Cackle	**Cackle Carlson**, born c.1882 (Rockford, Illinois, 1930 US census)
Chirp	**Chirp Buck**, born Prussia, c.1843 (Sycamore, Illinois, 1880 US census)
Choochoo	**Choochoo Hay**, born c.1888 (San Carlos, Arizona, 1896 US Indian census)

Chortle	**Chortle Ballard**, born North Carolina, 1865 (Catawba Springs, North Carolina, 1900 US census)
Chuckle	**Chuckle Jackson**, born Texas, 1881 (Longview, Texas, 1900 US census)
Clang	**Clang McMann**, born Ireland, c.1882 (Dallas, Iowa, 1910 US census)
Clap	**Clap Worton**, born Cradley, Worcestershire, c.1859 (Cradley, 1861 census)
Clash	**Clash Austin**, born St John's Wood, London, c.1863 (Lambeth, London, 1881 census)
Clatter	**Clatter Guffey**, born 26 March 1904; died Rutherfordton, North Carolina, USA, October 1974
Clink	**Clink A. Tabor Perkins**, born Pitcombe, Somerset, c.1891 (Wincanton, Somerset, 1901 census)
Clonk	**Clonk Sheppard**, born Florida, c.1903 (Pensacola, Florida, 1910 US census)
Cluck	**Cluck Benjamin**, born Pennsylvania, c.1831 (Jackson, Pennsylvania, 1870 US census)
Clunk	**Clunk Berger**, born Indiana, c.1888 (Frankfort, Indiana, 1920 US census)
Crackle	**Ellen Crackle Wagg**, born Derby, 1898
Crash	**Crash Kane**, born St Pancras, London, c.1885 (St Pancras, 1891 census)
Croak	**Croak Cresto**, born France, c.1826 (Hamilton, Ohio, 1860 US census)
	Croak Kate Fain, born New York, c.1862 (Orangeville, New York, 1930 US census)
Ding	**Ding Ding**, born 30 May 1971; died Thanet, Kent, 2001

Dong	**Dong Dong**, born 23 August 1968; died Thanet, Kent, 2001
Fizzy	**Fizzy Allgood**, died Daviess [*sic*], Kentucky, USA, 22 March 1922
Flash	**Flash Lancaster**, born 13 April 1918; died North Yorkshire, January 2001
Gabble	**Gabble Blanger**, born North Carolina, *c.*1815 (Craven, North Carolina, 1880 US census)
Gibber	**Gibber Williams**, born Aberdare, Glamorgan, *c.*1879 (Merthyr Tydfil, Glamorgan, 1891 Wales census)
Glug	**Glug Prue**, born Texas, 1897 (Dallas, Texas, 1900 US census)
Gnash	**Gnash Glidewell**, born South Carolina, *c.*1790 (Fairfield, Indiana, 1850 US census)
Grunt	**Grunt Little**, born South Carolina, *c.*1906 (New York, 1930 US census)
Gulp	**Gulp McKay**, born South Carolina, *c.*1882 (Red Springs, North Carolina, 1930 US census)
Gurgle	**Gurgle C. Harrison**, died Lambeth, London, 1962
Gush	**Gush Treakle**, born Germany, *c.*1861 (Merthyr Tydfil, Glamorgan, 1881 Wales census)
Hiss	**Hiss Morris**, born Newtown, Montgomeryshire, *c.*1877 (Newtown, 1891 Wales census)
Honk	**Honk Cockrane**, born Culross, Fife, *c.*1781 (St Pancras, London, 1861 census)
Hum	**Hum Knee**, born Gloucestershire, *c.*1811 (Stroud, Gloucestershire, 1841 England census)

Hush	**Hush Thrupp**, died Greenwich, London, 1919
Jabber	**Jabber Aid**, born 15 June 1894; died Alexandria, Virginia, USA, March 1967
Jangle	**Jangle Bowles**, born Pennsylvania, *c.*1846 (Montgomery, Pennsylvania, 1870 US census)

Jingle	**Jingle Jolly**, born South Carolina, 1885 (Effingham Township, South Carolina, 1900 US census)
Moo	**Moo Woodhead**, born Cleobury, Shropshire, *c*.1815 (Pershore, Worcestershire, 1851 census)
Munch	**Munch Wiley**, born 22 April 1885; died Memphis, Tennessee, USA, 15 April 1967
Oink	**Oink Adams**, born Mississippi, *c*.1855 (Quitman, Mississippi, 1920 US census)
Ping	**Ping Pong**, born China, *c*.1864 (San Francisco, California, 1910 US census)
Pop	**Pop Belcher**, born 22 January 1923; died Bristol, Gloucestershire, 2002
Puff	**Puff Finch**, born Alabama, 1870 (Franklin, Alabama, 1870 US census)
Purr	**Purr Peeples**, born Tennessee, *c*.1865 (Cannon, Tennessee, 1870 US census)
Quack	**Quack Pow**, born California, *c*.1875 (San Francisco, California, 1920 US census)
Rap	**Rap Smith**, born Doncaster, Yorkshire, 1900
Rattle	**Rattle Rattican**, died Ipswich, Suffolk, 1951
Rip	**Rip Van Wonkis**, born Germany, *c*.1844 (Holborn, London, 1871 census)
Scream	**Scream Marian**, born *c*.1880 (Henry, Kentucky, 1930 US census)
Screech	**Sarah Screech Clatworthy**, born St Germans, Cornwall, 1852
Shriek	**Shriek Kenedy** [*sic*], born Georgia, *c*.1879 (Brier Patch, Georgia, 1880 US census)
Sizzle	**Sizzle Poath**, born Missouri, *c*.1863 (Walnut, Missouri, 1880 US census)

Slap	**Slap Higgins**, born Texas, 1869 (Bell, Texas, 1900 US census)
Slosh	**Slosh Hirsh**, born Prussia, c.1835 (New York, 1880 US census)
Smack	**Smack Bolton**, born Kentucky, c.1891 (Franklin, Illinois, 1910 US census)
Smash	**Smash Spivey**, born Louisiana, c.1870 (Lincoln, Louisiana, 1880 US census)
Snap	**Snap Bean**, born 2 September 1914; died Luna, New Mexico, USA, January 1972
Sniff	**Sniff Bustomoff**, born Poland, c.1886 (Cuyahoga, Ohio, 1920 US census)
Sniffy	**Sniffy Tubbs**, born Texas, c.1878 (Montgomery, Texas, 1880 US census)
Snore	**Snore Annie Black**, born Bow, London, c.1867 (Chartham, Kent, 1891 census)
Snort	**Snort Dobson**, born Arkansas, c.1876 (Spring Hill, Arkansas, 1880 US census)
Sob	**Sob Rigsby**, born 10 February 1896; died Huntsville, Texas, USA, July 1974
Spit	**Spit Winkinson**, born Ohio, c.1823 (Laurel, Indiana, 1870 US census)
Splash	**Splash Carver**, born 1913; died Romsey, Hampshire, 2001
Sprinkle	**Sprinkle Ball**, born Pennsylvania, c.1873 (Elk Creek, Pennsylvania, 1880 US census)
Sputter	**Sputter Wilson**, born Georgia, c.1864 (Phillipsburg, Georgia, 1910 US census)
Squash	**Squash McDemon**, born Alabama, 1870 (James, Alabama, 1870 US census)

Squeak	**Linda Squeak Herman-Bourland**, born 8 July 1949; died 16 May 2004 (Black Hills National Cemetery, Sturgis, South Dakota, USA)
Squeal	**Squeal Miller**, born Tennessee, c.1904 (Martin, Tennessee, 1930 US census)
Squelch	**Samuel Squelch Shakespeare**, born Ashby-de-la-Zouch, Leicestershire, 1841
Squish	**Squish Smith**, born Florida, c.1847 (Sumter, Georgia, 1880 US census)
Swish	**Swish Raper**, born Ohio, c.1834 (Columbus, Ohio, 1910 US census)
Thud	**Thud Camel**, born Alabama, 1860 (Sumterville, Alabama, 1900 US census)
Thump	**Thump Stucky**, born Mississippi, c.1902 (Yazoo, Mississippi, 1920 US census)
Tinkle	**Richard Tinkle Bell**, born 22 December 1909; died Goole, Humberside, 1981
Titter	**Titter Pratt**, born Missouri, c.1872 (Lewis and Clark, Montana, 1910 US census)
Toot	**Toot Alice M. Hinkley**, born Faversham, Kent, 1878

Twang	**Twang Jones**, born West Virginia, 1898 (Clay, West Virginia, 1900 US census)
Tweet	**George Tweet Foster**, born Hartley Wintney, Hampshire, 1869
Vroom	**Vroom Posey**, born New Jersey, c.1828 (Montague, New Jersey, 1850 US census)
Whack	**Whack Crump**, born North Carolina, c.1904 (Boone, North Carolina, 1910 US census)
Wham	**Wham Swain**, born Topsham, Devon, c.1841 (Topsham, 1851 census)
Whimper	**George Whimper Lemon**, born East Bergholt, Suffolk, c.1844 (East Bergholt, 1851 census)
Whinny	**Whinny Barthrup**, baptized Gillingham, Kent, 18 June 1699
Whistle	**Whistle Bird**, born Indiana, c.1858 (Union, Indiana, 1870 US census)
Whiz(z)	**Whiz Horn**, born Georgia, c.1868 (Mount Zion, Georgia, 1870 US census)
	Whizz Moore, born North Carolina, c.1907 (Catawaba Springs, North Carolina, 1920 US census)
Woosh	**Woosh Hardy**, born South Carolina, c.1858 (Turkey Creek, South Carolina, 1870 US census)
Zap	**Zap Bullman**, born England, 1859 (York, Ontario, 1901 Canada census)
Zing	**Zing Moore**, born 30 December 1901; died Belmont, Ohio, USA, April 1977
Zonk	**Zonk Star**, born 9 October 1957; died Camden, London, 2004
Zoom	**Zoom Harris**, born Louisiana, c.1875 (Fort Bend, Texas, 1920 US census)

What a Mouthful!

Long and/or multiple names may perhaps derive from parental indecision when, given a list of options, they choose all of them, hence the child who received 138 first names (although how many she actually uses is anyone's guess). In alphabetical order, the names she was given are:

Abbie Adelaide Alanna Alexandra Alexandrina Alison Amanda Amy Anabel Andrea Angela Angelina Angie Anna Annabella Anne Annette Anthea Arabella Astrid Audry Ava Avril Barbara Bella Bernadette Beryl Beth Beverley Bonnie Bonny Brenda Bridget Camila Candice Candy Cara Carissa Carol Caroline Carrie Carrinna Cassie Catalina Catherine Cathlene Cecilia Charmaine Cheryl Christable Christine Clara Clarinda Clarissa Connie Constance Corina Crystal Cynthia Dana Daphne Dawn Debbie Dee Delilah Diana Donna Dorothy Eileen Elizabeth Elsie Emma Erika Felicity Fillippa Gabriella Geraldine Gina Grace Hazel Helen Hilary Honor Iris Isabella Jackie Jane Jean Jennifer Jessica Julie Karren Kate Kay Lena Lisa Louise Lynda Lynn Maggie Mandy Margaret Marian Mariclaire Melinda Miriam Moira Nancy Nichola Norma Pamela Patricia Pauline Penny Queenie Rebecca Rosemary Ruth Samantha Sandra Sara Selina Shari Susan Tammy Toni Tracy Ursula Valerie Vanessa Vicki Victoria Violet Vivien Wendy Zara Zoe Zsa Zsa

Other modern examples have included babies named after an entire Premier League football team – which, given the volatility of the transfer market, is doomed to ephemerality. Similarly, as recently as 2007, a family gave their daughter the names of 25 heavyweight boxing champions. They already had form – her mother had 26 names, her aunt 34 and her uncle bore the names of 42 bare-knuckle fighters.

Ann Bertha Cecilia Diana Emily Fanny Gertrude Hypatia Inez Jane Kate Louisa Maud Nora Ophelia Quince Rebecca Starkey Teresa Ulysis Venus Winifred Xenophen Yetty Zeus Pepper

Born West Derby, Lancashire, 19 December 1882. *She was given a name for each letter of the alphabet, in alphabetical order except that of her surname.*

Charles Caractacus Ostorius Maximillian Gustavus Adolphus Stone

Baptized Burbage, Wiltshire, 29 April 1781

Dancell Dallphebo Marc Antony Dallery Gallery Caesar Williams

Baptized Old Swinford, Worcestershire, 28 January 1676. *Son of Dancell Dallphebo Marc Antony Dallery Gallery Caesar Williams.*

Edith Kekuhikuhikuhipuuoneonaaliiokohala Kanaele Kanakaole

Born 30 October 1913; died Hilo, Hawaii, USA, October 1979. *She was an expert on Hawaiian culture and hula dancing.*

La Rhennee Le Veghonora Jannette Betsey Restall De Louth

Born Midhurst, Hampshire, 1850

Louis George Maurice Adolph Roch Albert Abel Antonio Alexandre Noë Jean Lucien Daniel Eugène Joseph-le-brun Joseph-Barême Thomas Thomas Thomas-Thomas Pierre Arbon Pierre-Maurel Barthélemi Artus Alphonse Bertrand Dieudonné Emanuel Josué Vincent Luc Michel Jules-de-la-Plane Jules-Bazin Julio César Jullien

> Born Siteron, France, 23 April 1812; died Neuilly-sur-Seine, France, 14 March 1860. *He was a French conductor and composer whose parents were persuaded by the thirty-six members of the Sisteron, France, Philharmonic Society that they should all be godfathers, and received all their names. He was usually known simply as 'The Maestro' (The Master).*

Luquincy Raine Martha Jane Eldorado Julie Dean Delma Ruthie Matilda Felma Jacka Cina Sophi Husky Charlotte Moss Stone Banks

> Born Alabama, c.1855 (Walker, Alabama, 1880 US census). *Known to her family and friends as Lu-Ma, she died aged 100 in Jasper, Alabama, USA.*

Mahershalalhashbaz Sturgeon

> Born Hessett, Suffolk, c.1857 (Hessett, 1881 census) *Mahershalalhashbaz is the longest personal name in the Bible.*

Maria de los Dolores Petrona Ramona Juana Nepomucena Josefa Cayetana Beatriz de la Santisima Trinidad North
> Born c.1811; died Lambeth, London, 1890

Shadrach Meshach Abednego Daniel Goldsmith
> Died Stow, Suffolk, 1849

Tilgathpilneser Smith
> Born Newmarket, Suffolk, 1861.
> *After Mahershalalhashbaz, Tilgathpilneser is one of the longest personal names in the Bible.*

Through-Much-Trial-and-Tribulation-We-Enter-The-Kingdom-of-Heaven Lindloff
> Born Iowa, 30 August 1880 (Clinton, Iowa, 1900 US census)

Xenia Marelina Veronique Caroline Sophia Murray Moore
> Born Richmond, Surrey, 1888

Xenophilus Epaphreditus Baycock Calvert
> Died Huddersfield, Yorkshire, 1842

Zaphnaphpanth Marker
> Born Nottingham, c.1811
> (Greasley, Nottinghamshire, 1841 census)

Zaphnathpaaneah Isaiah Obededom Nicodemus Francis Edward Clarke
> Baptized Beccles, Suffolk, 14 October 1804.
> *Only Francis Edward would fit in the parish register, so the other names were added as a footnote. In 1877 it was reported that 'Mr Zaphnath-Paaneah Isaiah Obed-Edom Nicodemus Francis Edward Clarke, a bloater merchant at Lowestoft, has been poisoned by taking a lotion in mistake for a draught.'*

The Tollemache-Tollemache family

The Reverend Ralph William Lyonel Tollemache (1826–1895), rector of South Wytham, near Grantham, Lincolnshire, established a unique place in British naming history by giving each of his 15 children both long and peculiar names. His first wife was his cousin Caroline Tollemache (1828–1867), with whom he had five children:

Lyonel Felix Carteret Eugene Tollemache (1854–1952)

Florence Caroline Artemisia Hume Tollemache (1855–1935)

Evelyne Clementina Wentworth Cornelia Maude Tollemache (1856–1919)

Granville Gray Marchmont Manners Plantagenet Tollemache (1858–1891)

Marchmont Murray Reginald Grasett Stanhope Plantagenet Tollemache (1860–1898). *Two years after the death of Caroline, Ralph married Dora Cleopatra Maria Lorenza de Orellana y Revest (c.1847–1929) and named their ten children in equally flamboyant style:*

Dora Viola Gertrude Irenez de Orellana Dysart Plantagenet Tollemache-Tollemache (1869–1874)

Mabel Helmingham Ethel Huntingtower Beatrice Blazonberrie Evangeline Vise de Lou de Orellana Plantagenet Saxon Toedmag Tollemache-Tollemache (1872–1955)

Lyonesse Matilda Dora Ida Agnes Ernestine Curson Paulet Wilbraham Joyce Eugénie Bentley Saxonia Dysart Plantagenet Tollemache-Tollemache (1874–1944)

Lyulph Ydwallo Odin Nestor Egbert Lyonel Toedmag Hugh Erchenwyne Saxon Esa Cromwell Orma Nevill Dysart Plantagenet Tollemache-Tollemache (1876–1961). *The initial letters of his first names spell 'Lyonel the Second'. He emigrated to New Zealand and continued the family tradition by having numerous children, although giving them less extravagant names than those of his siblings.*

Lyona Decima Veronica Esyth Undine Cyssa Hylda Rowena Viola Adela Thyra Ursula Ysabel Blanche Lelias Dysart Plantagenet Tollemache-Tollemache (1878–1962)

Leo Quintus Tollemache-Tollemache de Orellana Plantagenet Tollemache-Tollemache (1879–1914). *In 1908 he renounced all but the first and last of his names by deed poll. He was killed in the first year of World War I – an abbreviated version of his name is commemorated on the Menin Gate, Ypres, Belgium.*

Lyonella Fredegunda Cuthberga Ethelswytha Ideth Ysabel Grace Monica de Orellana Plantagenet Tollemache-Tollemache (1882–1952)

Leone Sextus Denys Oswolf Fraudatifilius Tollemache-Tollemache de Orellana Plantagenet Tollemache-Tollemache (1884–1917). *Like his brother Leo, Leone died in World War I.*

Lyonetta Edith Regina Valentine Myra Polwarth Avelina Philippa Violantha de Orellana Plantagenet Tollemache-Tollemache (1887–1951)

Lyonulph Cospatrick Bruce Berkeley Jermyn Tullibardine Petersham de Orellana Dysart Plantagenet Tollemache-Tollemache (1892–1966)

The All-Star Celebrity Baby Name Game

The mixed blessings of having a celebrity parent often begin in the cradle, as many have whacky names inflicted upon them. Award-winning film director Duncan Jones has proved it is possible to rise above a name conferred by a celebrity parent (in his case, by shedding his birth name of Zowie Bowie), and with any luck the rest of those that follow may survive and prosper despite their onomastic handicaps. I wish them well. By judiciously concealing either the names of the celebs or their unfortunate offspring, you can play the All-Star Celebrity Baby Name Game and guess who belongs to whom. Fun for all the family – except, perhaps, the kids in question.

Aanisah	Macy Gray & Tracy Hinds
Ahmet Emuukha Rodan	Frank & Adelaide Zappa
Amber Rose	Simon & Yasmin Le Bon
Apple	Chris Martin & Gwyneth Paltrow
Astrella Celeste	Donovan & Linda Lawrence
Atherton Grace	Don Johnson & Kelley Phleger
Atlas	Anne Heche & James Tupper
Audio Science	Shannyn Sossamon & Dallas Clayton
Aurelius Cy	Elle Macpherson & Arpad Busson

Bandit Lee	Lyn-Z & Gerard Way
Banjo Patrick	Rachel Griffiths & Andrew Taylor
Bardot Vita	Jaime Bergman & David Boreanaz
Beckett Robert Lee	Stella McCartney & Alasdhair Willis
Birdie West	Maura West & Scott DeFreitas
Blue Angel	The Edge & Aislinn O'Sullivan
Bluebell Madonna	Geri Halliwell
Bronx Mowgli	Ashlee Simpson-Wentz & Pete Wentz
Brooklyn	David & Victoria Beckham
Calico	Alice & Sheryl Cooper
Camera	Arthur Ashe & Jeanne Moutoussamy
Cash Anthony	Slash & Perla Ferrar
Charlie Tamara Tulip	Rebecca Romijn & Jerry O'Connell
Chastity	Cher & Sonny Bono
Coco Lux	Jo Whiley & Steve Morton
Cruz	David & Victoria Beckham
Daisy Boo	Jamie & Jules Oliver
Denim Cole	Toni Braxton & Keri Lewis
Destry	Steven Spielberg & Kate Capshaw
Diezel Ky	Toni Braxton & Keri Lewis
Diva Muffin	Frank & Adelaide Zappa
Dweezil	Frank & Adelaide Zappa
Elijah Blue	Cher & Greg Allman
Ella Blue	John Travolta & Kelly Preston
Eric Mustard	Helen Baxendale & David Williams

Fifi Trixibelle	Bob Geldof & Paula Yates
Fuchsia	Sting & Frances Tomelty
Gaia	Emma Thompson & Greg Wise
God'Iss Love Stone	Lil' Mo & Al Stone
Gulliver	Gary Oldman & Donya Fiorentino
Harlow Winter Kate	Nicole Richie & Joel Madden
Heaven Love'on Stone	Lil' Mo & Al Stone
Heavenly Hiraani Tiger Lily	Michael Hutchence & Paula Yates
Homer James Jigme	Richard Gere & Carey Lowell
Homer	Matt & Deborah Groening
Hopper	Sean Penn & Robin Wright
Hud	John Cougar Mellencamp
Ireland	Alec Baldwin & Kim Basinger
Jaden Gil	Steffi Graf & Andre Agassi
Jaz	Steffi Graf & Andre Agassi
Jermajesty	Jermaine Jackson & Alejandra Genevieve Oaziaza
John Buffalo	Norman & Norris Mailer
Journey Jette & Jesse (twins)	Jenna Jameson & Tito Ortiz
Kal-El Coppola	Nicholas & Alice Cage
Kyd	David Duchovny & Tea Leoni
Lark Song	Mia Farrow & André Previn
Lennon	Liam Gallagher & Patsy Kensit
Liberty Beau	Ryan Giggs & Stacey Cooke
Lolita	Shane & Christie Richie

London Emilio	Slash & Perla Ferrar
Lourdes Maria	Madonna & Carlos Leon
Luna Coco Patricia	Frank Lampard & Elen Rives
Marquise	50 Cent & Shaniqua Tompkins
Mars Merkaba	Erykah Badu & Jay Electronica
Mason Dash	Kourtney Kardashian & Scott Disick
Max Liron	Christina Aguilera & Jordan Bratman
Memphis Eve	Bono & Alison Hewson
Moon Unit	Frank & Adelaide Zappa
Moxie CrimeFighter	Penn & Emily Jillette
Nahla Ariela	Halle Berry & Gabriel Aubry
Neil Marmalade	Helen Baxendale & David Williams
Nyiema	Lemar & Charmaine Powell
Oriole Nebula	Donovan & Linda Lawrence
Peaches Honeyblossom	Bob Geldof & Paula Yates
Petal Blossom Rainbow	Jamie & Jules Oliver
Phoenix Chi	Mel B & Jimmy Gulzar
Pilot Inspektor	Jason Lee & Beth Riesgraf
Piper Maru	Gillian Anderson & Clyde Klotz
Pixie	Bob Geldof & Paula Yates
Poppy Honey	Jamie & Jules Oliver
Prince Michael	Michael Jackson
Princess Tiaamii	Katie Price & Peter Andre
Puma Sabti	Erykah Badu & The D.O.C.

Racer Maximilliano	Robert & Elizabeth Rodriguez
Rebel Antonio	
Rocket Valentino	
Rogue Joaquin	
Romeo	David & Victoria Beckham
Rufus Tiger	Roger & Debbie Taylor
Rumer Glenn	Bruce Willis & Demi Moore
Saffron Sahara	Simon & Yasmin Le Bon
Sage Florence	Toni Collette & Dave Galafassi
Sage Moonblood	Sylvester Stallone & Sasha Czack
Sam Bazooka	Elliot & Jennifer Gould
Satchel	Spike Lee & Tonya Lewis Lee
Satchel	Woody Allen & Mia Farrow
Scout LaRue	Bruce Willis & Demi Moore
Seargeoh	Sylvester Stallone & Sasha Czack
Seven Sirius	Andre Benjamin & Erykah Badu
Shiloh Nouvel	Brad Pitt & Angelina Jolie
Sonnet	Forest & Keisha Whitaker
Sonora Rose	Alice & Sheryl Cooper
Sosie	Kevin Bacon & Kyra Sedgwick
Sparrow James Midnight	Nicole Richie & Joel Madden
Speck Wildhorse	John Cougar Mellencamp
Sunday Rose	Nicole Kidman & Keith Urban
Suri	Tom Cruise & Katie Holmes
Tahmel	Macy Gray & Tracy Hinds
Tallulah Belle	Bruce Willis & Demi Moore

Tallulah Pine	Simon & Yasmin Le Bon
Tara Gabriel Galaxy Gramophone	Sir John Paul & Talitha Getty
Tiger Lily	Roger & Debbie Taylor
True	Forest & Keisha Whitaker
Vincent Mash	Helen Baxendale & David Williams
Willow Camille Reign	Will Smith & Jada Pinkett-Smith
Zola Ivy	Eddie Murphy & Nicole Mitchell
Zolten	Penn & Emily Jillette
Zowie	David & Angela Bowie
Zum a Nesta Rock	Gwen Stefani & Gavin Rossdale

7. My New Name Is...

Of course, when all is said and done, you can always change your name – as many of those listed in the preceding pages perhaps wisely did. Although extreme examples are often the subject of press features today, name changes are not a modern phenomenon: Joshua Bug's decision to change his name to Norfolk Howard was announced in *The Times* on 26 June 1862. John Robert Shittler, born in 1851 in Wimborne, Dorset, married Martha Reeve in Kingston, Surrey, in 1877. She survived seven years of marriage as Mrs Shittler, but must have been relieved when, in 1884, her husband changed the family name to Rowden; and, famously, the Battenbergs transmogrified into the Mountbattens during World War I, while British people who found themselves with the surnames Hitler or Goering did the same in World War II. But name-changing is not all plain sailing: as a final note of caution and an awful warning, consider some of the self-inflicted names that people in the UK and beyond have come up with in recent years. Some deed poll name changes were unsurprisingly drink-related or the outcome of a bet (presumably one they lost), and in many instances resulted in family strife and practical problems, such as the refusal of the Identity and Passport Service to issue a passport in the adopted name.

Aerial Sparks
    Andrew Biddulph, London, 2005

**Ant Level Forty Two The Pursuit Of Accidents The
Early Tapes Standing In The Light True Colours A
Physical Presence World Machine Running in the
Family Running In The Family Platinum Edition Staring
At The Sun Level Best Guaranteed The Remixes Forever
Now Influences Changes Mark King Mike Lindup Phil
Gould Boon Gould Wally Badarou Lindup-Badarou**
    The rock group Level 42 fan formerly known as
    Antony Hicks of Truro, Cornwall, who in 1994
    changed his name into a list of the band's original
    line-up and its record releases.

**Aron Mufasa Columbo Fonzarelli Ball In Acup Boogie
Woogie Brown**
    Aron Brown, Derby, 2008

Aston Martin
    Alan Tunnard, Southampton, Hampshire, 2009

Ava Truly Scrumptious
    Ava Payne, Banbury, Oxfordshire, 2009

Big Crazy Lester
    Joel Whittle, Blackpool, Lancashire, 2007

**Captain Fantastic Faster Than Superman Spiderman
Batman Wolverine The Hulk And The Flash Combined**
    George Garratt, Glastonbury, Somerset, 2008

Chainey Rabbit
    Jermaine Harris, Kent, 2006

Dady Fantastic
    Robert Sullivan, Stroud, Gloucestershire, 2007

Dan Boombastic Fantastic
    Daniel Adshead, Dukinfield, Cheshire, 2006

Elf McGnome
    George Smith, Middlesex, 2006

General Ninja Ant
   Anthony Richard Giles
   Bailey, Southend-on-Sea,
   Essex, 2008

GoldenPalace.com
   In 2005, the Montreal
   casino paid Terri Iligan
   $15,199 to change her
   name.

Happy Adjustable Spanners
   Daniel Westfallen,
   Hornchurch, Essex,
   2008

Hayley Comet
   Hayley Williams, Paignton,
   Devon, 2005

HMP Holloway
   Samantha Holloway,
   Canning Town, London,
   2007

Honey Monster
   Peter Thomas, Brighton, East Sussex, 2008

Hong Kong Phooey
   Gary Brett, Potters Bar, Hertfordshire, 2002

Jam Danger Sponge
   Jamie Lambe, Leeds, Yorkshire, 2007

Jellyfish McSaveloy
   Steven Lane, Beeston, Nottinghamshire, 2005

Jo Jo Magicspacemonkey
   Rhys Jones, Denbighshire, 2006

Lucy O Loquette
   Katherine Neill, Malmesbury, Wiltshire, 2005

Martin Felix Oddsocks McWeirdo El-Tooty Fruity Farto Hello Hippopotamus Bum
   Formerly Martin Felix Smith

Motherwell Football Club
Frazer Boyle, Coltness, Lanarkshire, 2009

Mouth Who Wants To Know O'Mighty
Chris Gray, Bingley, West Yorkshire, 2007

Nigel Bottomface
Shaun Henessey, South Woodham Ferrers, Essex, 2005

Nineteen Sixty-Eight
Claire Turney, London, 2005

None Of The Above
Adam Neil Osen, Chingford, Essex, 2009

**N'Tom The Hayemaker
Haywardyoulkiketocomebacktomine**
Tom Hayward, Market Harborough, Leicestershire,
2008

Purple Phantom
Peter Bensted, Stepney, London, 2006

Rhyme-Master Joey Joe Joe Toasterface
David Baird, Dartford, Kent, 2004

Richard Oldham Athletic Metcalfe
Richard Metcalfe, Oldham, Lancashire, 2005

Saxon Knight
Janice Gover, Exmouth, Devon, 2008

Sin D'rella
Sharon Jordan, Mitcham, Surrey, 2005

Solar Fruitbat Samba
Roger Donkin, Coventry, Warwickshire, 2005

Something Long And Complicated
William Wood, Scunthorpe, Lincolnshire, 2007

Supa Hereo Vez
Ross James Verrall, Reading, Berkshire, 2005

**Tarquin Fin-tim-lim-bim-whin-bim-lim-bus-stop-
F'tang-F'tang-Olè-Biscuitbarrel**
John Desmond Lewis, Hayes, London, 1979

The Boy Flood
Paul Francis, Tiverton, Devon, 2005

Tim Mind Your Own Business And Kiss My Arsenal Swain
Tim Swain, Letchworth, Hertfordshire, 2005

Tintin Captain Haddock Confused Brewer
Chris Brewer, Leeds, Yorkshire, 2008

Toasted T Cake
Nigel Doyle, Manchester, 2005

Trout Fishing in America
Formerly Peter John Eastman of Carpinteria, California, USA, he changed his name in 1994 to the title of Richard Brautigan's 1967 cult novella.

Will Funk-Dog Perez
William Scott Bryan, Staffordshire, 2009

Yahoo Serious
Born Greg Pead, the Australian actor who starred in *Young Einstein* changed his name in 1980.

Yellow-Rat Foxysquirrel Fairydiddle
Richard James, St Albans, Hertfordshire, 2002

The End

Acknowledgements

Thanks to all the archivists and others with an eye for strange names who have so generously been feeding them to me since I tackled my first book on the subject, *Potty, Fartwell & Knob*. My appetite for them remains unsated, so if you were at school with, worked with, are related to or even just know about someone with a memorable name – provided it can be verified and is not just something you heard in the pub – please contact me at www.russellash.com.